SHIBE PARK–
CONNIE MACK
STADIUM

FRONT COVER: Danny Litwhiler was a hard-hitting Phillies left fielder from 1940 to 1943 during an 11-year career in the major leagues. In 1942, he became the first outfielder in big-league history to play an entire season without making an error. Ultimately, Litwhiler played errorless ball in 187 straight games. He was also noted as a highly successful college coach and an innovator, author, and inventor. (Author's collection.)

COVER BACKGROUND: Shibe Park, later renamed Connie Mack Stadium, housed major-league baseball and a variety of other sports from 1909 through 1970. It was the home of the Philadelphia Athletics for 46 years and the Phillies for 32 and a half seasons. (Author's collection.)

BACK COVER: Future Hall of Famers Robin Roberts (left) and Richie Ashburn (right) were two mainstays of the Phillies when they won the National League pennant in 1950. Known as the Whiz Kids, the team was led by manager Eddie Sawyer (center) and won the flag on the last day of the season on Dick Sisler's 10th-inning, three-run homer against the Brooklyn Dodgers at Ebbets Field. (Author's collection.)

SHIBE PARK–
CONNIE MACK
STADIUM

Rich Westcott

ARCADIA
PUBLISHING

Copyright © 2012 by Rich Westcott
ISBN 978-1-5316-5067-4

Published by Arcadia Publishing
Charleston, South Carolina

Library of Congress Control Number: 2011929590

For all general information, please contact Arcadia Publishing:
Telephone 843-853-2070
Fax 843-853-0044
E-mail sales@arcadiapublishing.com
For customer service and orders:
Toll-Free 1-888-313-2665

Visit us on the Internet at www.arcadiapublishing.com

This book is dedicated to Adrienne and Georgia,
two new and very special members of the family

CONTENTS

ACKNOWLEDGMENTS

There were a number of significant contributors to the pages of this book, all of whom deserve a special thank you from the author. Particularly helpful was Bob Warrington, whose time, expertise, and photographic contributions were invaluable. The author also wants to thank Brenda Galloway-Wright of the Urban Archives at Temple University, Tim Wiles of the Baseball Hall of Fame, Jim Gallagher, Chuck Hasson, Bill White, and the author's son Chris Westcott, whose assistance in various ways knew no bounds. Their help was vital to the completion of this project.

Unless otherwise credited, all pictures came from the collection of the author. A key source was his book *Philadelphia Old Ballparks*, published in 1996 by Temple University Press.

INTRODUCTION

Long before Shibe Park became one of the most storied venues in Philadelphia history, baseball had become the city's most popular sport, with ballparks scattered throughout the area.

Variations of baseball games were first known to have been played in Philadelphia in the early 1830s. As the 19th century progressed, an increasing number of teams appeared throughout the area, so that just prior to the start of the Civil War more than 100 club teams existed.

In 1865, a team called the Athletics signed one of baseball's first professional players, a left-handed second baseman who was born in England named Al Reach. Paid $1,000 for the season, he later became the founder and first owner of the Phillies.

By the late 1860s, African American teams, as well as additional club teams, had formed. In 1871, the Athletics became one of the original teams in the National Association of Professional Baseball Players and won the first championship of baseball's first professional league. Five years later, another team called the Athletics became a charter member of the new National League. The first NL game, which pitted the Athletics and the Boston Red Caps, was played in 1876 in Philadelphia at Jefferson Park at Twenty-fifth and Jefferson Streets. Jefferson Park—or Athletic Park as it was sometimes called—was the city's first fully enclosed ball field.

By then, there were a number of other baseball parks, including Columbia Park at Fifteenth Street and Columbia Avenue, Oakdale Park at Eleventh and Cumberland Streets, Keystone Park at Broad and Moore Streets, and Forepaugh Park at Broad and Dauphin Streets. Over the years, the fields were used by a variety of Philadelphia professional teams. Sometimes, as many as three games, one from each league, were taking place—all within a few blocks of each other.

When the Phillies were formed in 1883, they played at Recreation Park at Ridge and Columbia Avenues and Twenty-fourth and Twenty-fifth Streets. The ballpark had existed since 1860 and was the site of Philadelphia's first recorded baseball game, a slugfest in which a team called Equity walloped one called the Pennsylvanias, 65-52.

After four seasons there, the Phillies built a new park at Broad Street and Lehigh Avenue that was originally called Philadelphia Base Ball Park. Later, the name was changed to Baker Bowl. The Phillies, the fourth-oldest team in the major leagues, spent 51 and a half years at Baker Bowl before moving to Shibe Park in the middle of the 1938 season.

Meanwhile, the American League had formed in 1901, and another team called the Athletics was one of the league's original members. They played at another Columbia Park, this one located at Twenty-ninth Street and Columbia Avenue.

Columbia Park was the home of pennant-winning Athletics teams in 1902 and 1905 and one World Series team in 1905. But with a meager capacity of just 9,500, it was not big enough to handle the crowds that followed the increasingly popular Athletics.

A new ballpark was needed. Ben Shibe, who owned 50 percent of the Athletics stock (Connie Mack owned 25 percent), had the perfect spot. It was a vacant 250,120-square-foot lot at Twenty-first Street and Lehigh Avenue in what was then a thinly populated section of the city near neighborhoods known as Swampoodle and Goosetown.

Seven blocks up Lehigh Avenue from the Phillies' Philadelphia Base Ball Park (or Huntingdon Grounds as it was also called), the land was neither close to center city nor in an area that had much activity. The most prominent landmark was the Philadelphia Hospital for Contagious Diseases, which stood across the street from the future ballpark and was noted for treating smallpox cases. Although isolated from much of the city's 1.5 million people and 25 blocks from center city, the mostly undeveloped area was accessible by several trolley lines, a condition that, despite some reservations, convinced the Athletics owners the land was a worthwhile purchase.

Through a complicated set of financial maneuvers, Shibe and his partners formed the Athletic Grounds Company and purchased the land in 1908 for $141,918.92. Soon, construction was underway. It took two months to grade the land with 40 workers and 50 teams of horses hauling in 15,000 wagonloads of dirt, much of it imported from Columbia Park. More than 500 tons of steel were poured into the structural sections of the ballpark, making it the first steel-and-concrete stadium in the country.

The ballpark was built by the William Steele and Sons construction company at a cost to the Athletics of $315,248.69. Completed in less than one year, it had an ornate facade with a French Renaissance motif. The outside featured brick walls and arched windows bordered by thick columns. An imposing domed tower dominated the main entrance to the ballpark at Twenty-first Street and Lehigh Avenue. The capacity was 23,000, although another 1,000 could stand behind ropes on a banked terrace that ran across the outfield. A garage that could hold 200 cars stood beneath the stands along Lehigh Avenue.

Upper and lower decks ran from third base to first base. The lower deck stretched down the foul lines to the outfield walls. There was no grandstand in the outfield. A 12-foot-high wall stretched from left field to right. It was 515 feet from home plate to center field, 378 feet down the left-field line, and 340 feet to the wall in right field.

The ballpark was named Shibe Park after its primary owner, a one-time trolley-car driver and mechanic who had become owner of a sporting-goods manufacturing company that in 1883 had been credited with developing the cork-centered baseball.

When it was opened in 1909, Shibe Park was regarded as the finest ballpark in the nation. The new facility was considered a showpiece, and people from far and wide flocked to see it. Shibe Park was so well received, in fact, that within five years of its opening, 10 other new parks were built.

Shibe Park would be eventually renamed Connie Mack Stadium. It was home to the Athletics for 46 seasons and the Phillies for 32 and a half years and was the home of the Philadelphia Eagles from 1940 to 1957. Countless Negro League games were played there, and it was the site of legions of college and high school football and baseball games, plus a huge assortment of other sporting and non-sporting events.

During Shibe Park's 62 years of existence, some 47 million fans watched big-league baseball games there. Eight World Series, seven involving the Athletics, were played there. So were two All-Star Games. The first American League night game was played at Shibe Park. It was visited by two standing US presidents.

Twenty-first and Lehigh—to more than four generations of baseball devotees, it was an address that was one of the most familiar in the entire Philadelphia area. Everyone knew what was there. Everyone had a special story about it. Once the hub of the area's sports world, it held a special place in the hearts and minds of the area's baseball fans. Even today, Shibe Park ranks prominently in Philadelphia baseball history, its legendary past celebrated whenever old ballparks are discussed.

IN THE BEGINNING

The date of April 12, 1909, has forever stood as one of the most significant days in Philadelphia baseball history. It was the day that Shibe Park opened.

Fans began lining up for tickets at 7:00 a.m., five hours before the gates opened and eight hours before game time. More than 35,000 people, some 12,000 above the capacity of the ballpark and including scores of dignitaries, got in. An estimated 30,000 more jammed outside the park, many on the roofs of nearby houses and some in trees or on the tops of carriages. Eventually, after Mayor John Reyburn threw out the first ball and second baseman Amby McConnell became the first batter, lefthander Eddie Plank tossed a six-hitter as the Athletics defeated the Boston Red Sox, 8-1.

The day was not without tragedy. Following the game, A's catcher Michael "Doc" Powers was rushed to the hospital with an intestinal problem. Afterward, his condition steadily deteriorated, and despite three operations, Powers died two weeks later.

But the otherwise extraordinary day was a sign of things to come. The Athletics drew 674,915 fans—more than 200,000 above their best year at Columbia Park and a team mark that stood until 1925. And they would win four pennants in the next five years and claim World Series victories in 1910, 1911, and 1913.

With lineups that included future Hall of Famers Eddie Collins, Frank "Home Run" Baker, Plank, Rube Waddell, and Charles Albert "Chief" Bender, the Athletics were the toast of the town. And Shibe Park was such a success that within the next five years, 10 more new big-league ballparks made of steel and concrete were built.

As Shibe Park's popularity increased, so did that of the surrounding area. Farms and scattered housing gave way to streets lined with row homes. Stores, small businesses, and churches proliferated, catering to the various ethnic groups—primarily English, Italian, German, and Irish—that had moved in. And a variety of manufacturers located their plants in the area, taking advantage of the local working-class population.

Increased public transportation, including a trolley line that stretched down Lehigh Avenue, made the ballpark more accessible. With a train stop nearby at North Broad Street Station, which was also used by the teams as they arrived and departed from the city, fans flocked to the ballpark. It was not unusual for an A's game to attract as many as 30,000 spectators.

From 1901, when the American League began, through the 1908 season, the Athletics played at Columbia Park at Twenty-ninth Street and Columbia Avenue in the Brewerytown section of Philadelphia. Built at a cost of $35,000, the ballpark had a seating capacity of 9,500. The A's won two pennants while playing there and lost the 1905 World Series in five games to the New York Giants. All five games, including the two played at Columbia Park, were shutouts, with Christy Mathewson pitching three of them.

A ground-breaking ceremony for Shibe Park was held in 1908 with Athletics and city officials in attendance. Among the dignitaries were Tom Shibe (far left), Ben Shibe (third from left), Connie Mack (sixth from left), and John Shibe (fourth from right).

IN THE BEGINNING

Opened in 1909, Shibe Park dominated the area around Twenty-first Street and Lehigh Avenue. The huge building with the colorful redbrick facade featured an imposing domed tower at the main entrance. Connie Mack's ornately furnished office was located at the top of the tower. Reached by a runway that extended from the upper pavilion, it was flanked by several other offices that housed various Athletics executives.

Big crowds flocked to Shibe Park, regarded as the finest stadium in the country, to see the Athletics play. Fans standing along Lehigh Avenue waited in long lines to enter the park through one of 16 turnstiles. Stores and restaurants also stood on the inside corridor along Lehigh Avenue.

In the first game played at Shibe Park, future Hall of Famer Eddie Plank yielded six hits, struck out eight, and walked four to lead the Athletics to an 8-1 victory over the Boston Red Sox. While he was with the A's, Plank won 20 or more games seven times during a 17-year career in which he won 327 games. In a 1912 game at Shibe Park, Plank pitched all 19 innings in a 5-4 loss to the Washington Senators. Walter Johnson got the win after working the final 10 innings in relief. (Baseball Hall of Fame Library.)

Philadelphia baseball fans were always a loud group that sometimes got out of control. A team of 16 special officers was always on hand at Athletics games to help keep the crowd in line. Their main duties including breaking up fights, putting drunk fans out of the park, ejecting those who threw objects onto the field, and trying to stop gambling in the stands. They carried billy clubs for needed enforcement. (Robert D. Warrington.)

When it was built, Shibe Park featured lower and upper decks that ran down the first- and third-base lines. An uncovered lower deck continued down the right- and left-field lines. There were seats for 23,000 spectators.

A special program was published on the day the Athletics honored former catcher Michael "Doc" Powers, who had died on April 26, 1909, after playing in the first game at Shibe Park. Except for a brief stint with the New York Highlanders in 1905, Powers had been an A's catcher since the team was formed in 1901. (Robert D. Warrington.)

Trolleys traveling up and down Lehigh Avenue were the main form of transportation to early games at Shibe Park. The sign on the cowcatcher reads, "Base Ball Today at Shibe Park." (Robert D. Warrington.)

The Athletics' first power hitter was third baseman Frank "Home Run" Baker. On May 29, 1909, in his rookie season, he hit the first home run at Shibe Park, a drive over the right-field wall in the first game of a doubleheader with the Boston Red Sox. Baker went on to win four straight American League home runs crowns between 1911 and 1914 with totals ranging from 9 to 12. He also led the league twice in RBI during a career that led to the Hall of Fame. (Baseball Hall of Fame Library.)

With a crowd of 26,891 in attendance, some sitting on the field in front of the outfield walls, the Athletics' Eddie Collins got the first hit in the 1910 World Series. The A's went on to win their first World Series and the first one played at Shibe Park, beating the Chicago Cubs in five games.

Fans came to ball games at Shibe Park dressed in their finest clothing. In the bleachers, where fans sat on long planks of pinewood, a crowd made up almost exclusively of male fans wore coats, ties, and hats while attending the first game of the 1910 World Series. Men were expected to be properly attired, including covering their heads in public. (Robert D. Warrington.)

Eddie Collins making Philadelphia's first hit

Although it was empty in March, Shibe Park would soon be packed as fans flocked to the field to watch the Athletics win their second straight American League pennant and World Series in 1911. This time, the A's beat the New York Giants in six games. (Robert D. Warrington.)

SH_BE PARK · 9-1-1?
WASHINGTON GAME

Athletics players head to the dugout between innings of a game against the Washington Senators. The A's dugout was on the third-base side of the field. Behind the dugout, an enclosed runway took players up a ramp to the home-team locker room. (Robert D. Warrington.)

Fans congregated at the corner of Twenty-first Street and Lehigh Avenue, where the main entrance to Shibe Park was located. Once inside, fans could walk down a 14-foot-wide promenade that led to the bleachers or climb a grand stairway to the main grandstands. Vendors were scattered around the inside of the main entrance. (Baseball Hall of Fame and Library.)

In their early years, the Athletics used stationery that showed a front view of Shibe Park.

The right-field grandstands are seen here packed for an Athletics World Series game in 1911. Across Twentieth Street, rooftop seats were as yet not heavily used. Factories, as shown in the background, were scattered around the area of the ballpark. (Dennis Goldstein.)

The pre-game ceremony on opening day in 1912 included A's and Washington Senators players marching back to their dugouts after the US flag was raised in center field. One year later, the left-field wall along Somerset Street was removed and replaced by bleachers that extended to center field. (Robert D. Warrington.)

Interior Shibe Park Ball Grounds, Philadelphia, Pa.

This 1912 view of the interior of Shibe Park looking across the field to the left-field line was taken just one year before roofs were constructed atop the uncovered bleachers down the left- and right-field lines. At this point, the capacity of the ballpark was 23,000, but as many as 1,000 more fans sometimes stood behind ropes across the outfield. Police stood in front of the stands to keep order. (Robert D. Warrington.)

There was a packed house for the second game of the 1913 World Series pitting the Athletics against the New York Giants. Over a five-year period between 1910 and 1914, the Athletics appeared in four World Series, winning three of them. They won the 1913 series four games to one.

One of the most notable features of the early Athletics was what became known as "The $100,000 Infield." The name originated from the premise that the group was worth well beyond that sum. Danny Murphy (center) was a second baseman but had been shifted to the outfield when the legendary infield was formed. It consisted of (from left to right) second baseman Eddie Collins, shortstop Jack Barry, third baseman Frank Baker, and first baseman Stuffy McInnis. (Robert D. Warrington.)

One of three Athletics pitchers from the early years who made the Hall of Fame (Eddie Plank and Rube Waddell were the others), Charles Albert "Chief" Bender fired the first no-hitter at Shibe Park. It came on May 12, 1910, against the Cleveland Naps. Bender had a 23-5 record that year, his best during a 15-year career in the majors. Bender also recorded the first A's World Series victory at Shibe Park with a three-hit 4-1 win over the Chicago Cubs in 1910. (Robert D. Warrington.)

2

NOTHING EVER
STAYS THE SAME

No matter what it is, no entity ever stays the same. Shibe Park was no exception. The ballpark—and the team that played there—constantly underwent changes.

The Athletics went from good to atrocious. The shift began when Connie Mack broke up his perennial pennant winners, selling off the top players. Accordingly, the A's fell to the pits of the American League, finishing in last place seven straight seasons between 1915 and 1921 while losing 100 or more games five times, including 117 in 1916.

The population around Shibe Park, in an area then known as North Penn, continued to expand as more houses and factories were built. A block of row houses was built behind the left-field wall along Somerset Street, and another row of homes arose across Twentieth Street behind the right-field wall. Across the street, where the contagious-disease hospital stood until it was demolished in 1909 and where people walked past with handkerchiefs covering their mouths, a park was built. It was named Reyburn Park after Philadelphia's mayor.

Another landmark surfaced around that time when Matt Kilroy, a major-league player in the late 1800s who was a native Philadelphian and the great-uncle of future Philadelphia Eagles star Bucko Kilroy, opened a bar at Twentieth Street and Lehigh Avenue. Called Kilroy's Bar, it became a popular place for players and fans both before and after games. Kilroy sold it in 1935, and the bar's name was changed to Charlie Quinn's Deep Right Field Café. Often, it was used during games by players who would dash over from the right-field bullpen for a quick beer or sandwich.

Many Athletics players, as well as Mack, lived in the area, usually walking to the park followed by a crowd of neighborhood children. But attendance at games was paltry; one game drew just 300 spectators. Often, gamblers and assorted other unsavory characters comprised a large segment of the crowd.

The ballpark itself underwent numerous changes. In 1913, roofs were installed across the uncovered bleachers down the first- and third-base lines, and bleachers across the outfield from left to center were built. In 1925, upper decks were built over the stands down the first- and third-base lines at a cost of $400,000. Then, in 1928, a 750-seat mezzanine between the upper and lower decks behind home plate was added. The following year, 3,500 seats were added to the stands.

Shibe Park's most unforgettable look was the view at Twenty-first Street and Lehigh Avenue. Two ticket entrances stood on each side of the tower; players usually left the ballpark through those entrances. A chartered bus that carried players from visiting teams to their downtown hotels stood near the Lehigh Avenue entrance.

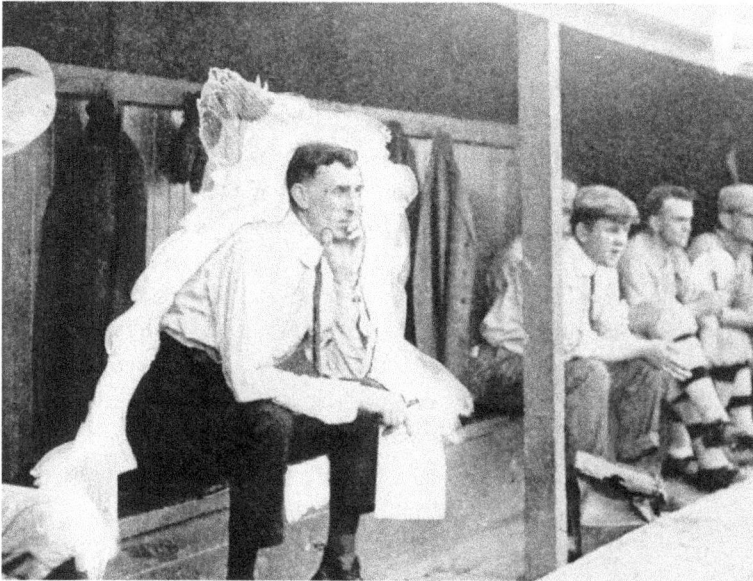

Throughout his career with the Athletics, Connie Mack always dressed in street clothes. In a characteristic pose, Mack sits in the team's third-base dugout with his scorecard poised to wave players into position.

Especially during big games and World Series contests, Twentieth Street was alive with activity in the early years. Hundreds of people sat on rooftops to watch games, while others looked out of upstairs windows or walked the street in search of a good spot to view the action.

In its early years, Shibe Park crowds consisted mostly of well-dressed men, some of whom rode to the game in fancy cars. This is a view of the ballpark along Twenty-first Street looking toward Somerset Street.

In an early A's game, as many as 1,000 fans could watch the action while standing or seated in front of the 12-foot-high right-field wall that stood along Twentieth Street. Some fans were actually on the playing field standing behind a temporary wooden fence.

The first-base side of Shibe Park stretched along Lehigh Avenue. Windows at the top level were located at the back of the upstairs grandstand.

There was no press box when Shibe Park was first opened. Well-dressed reporters from the city's nine daily newspapers sat at tables in the front two field-level rows of the stands. Small, hand-operated Teletype machines were used to send in the reports to the home office. The stories were vastly different from those written in today's publications.

After Connie Mack dissolved the Athletics dynasty, the team finished in last place seven straight times between 1915 and 1921, losing as many as 117 games in 1916. That season, the team's shortstop was a 20-year-old rookie named Whitey Witt. Later moved to the outfield, the youngster was a fixture with the A's for five seasons before being traded to the New York Yankees, where in 1923 he became the first Yankee to bat and to score a run in the brand-new Yankee Stadium.

On the day of a game, trolleys were packed with fans traveling along Lehigh Avenue to the ballpark. Trolleys ran in both directions and connected with the Broad Street subway after it was opened in 1924.

Shibe Park had a wide-open look across the outfield in its early years. Bleachers in left field were added to the ballpark in 1913.

NOTHING EVER STAYS THE SAME

The only time a no-hitter was pitched against the Athletics at Shibe Park was in 1923, when two no-hitters were hurled against them in the same week. Sam Jones did it first on September 4 pitching for the New York Yankees, and then three days later, Howard Ehmke repeated the feat while pitching for the Boston Red Sox. Ehmke (pictured) later joined the A's and in a legendary game was a surprise starter in the 1929 World Series opener. Recording the last victory of his career, Ehmke struck out a then-series record 13 while beating the Chicago Cubs, 3-1.

In 1925, an upper deck was built above the grandstands down the first- and third-base lines, giving fans in the lower deck some protection against bad weather. During games, police and newspaper photographers stood in foul territory against the wall.

Often called the greatest second baseman of all time, Eddie Collins began his career with the Athletics in 1906, playing through 1914, before returning to the club in 1927, finishing his playing days in 1930. No one appreciated Collins's talent more than Connie Mack.

Fans loitering in Reyburn Park across Lehigh Avenue and cars in front of Shibe Park were familiar sights before Athletics games in the 1920s. (Bill White.)

NOTHING EVER STAYS THE SAME

On a chilly day in September, fans are seen wearing overcoats as they are perched on roofs of houses behind the right-field wall along Twentieth Street. They climbed out of second-floor windows to reach the roofs. Some fans went up ladders to the top roofs. In any case, fans here watched games without paying an admission fee to the Athletics. There was always room on the rooftops for spectators, who paid nominal fees to the homeowners and climbed to their lofty perches on ladders, some that went up through the transoms located in upstairs bathrooms. Even women occasionally climbed to the rooftops.

Both Ty Cobb (left) and Nap Lajoie (below) ended their careers playing with the Athletics. The future Hall of Famers, each of who entered Cooperstown in the first year inductees were admitted (1939), both spent two years with the A's. In Cobb's next-to-last year (1927), he hit .357 as the club's regular right fielder.

3

A WHOLE NEW LOOK

During the 1920s and 1930s, a lot was happening at Twenty-first Street and Lehigh Avenue.

In 1928, a subway that stretched from Philadelphia City Hall to Olney Avenue was opened. For 8¢, fans could ride the subway the three miles to Lehigh Avenue, then walk or hop a trolley the seven more blocks to the ballpark.

The following year, the Athletics began a run of three straight trips to the World Series, winning the first two. With a new group of future Hall of Famers, including Jimmie Foxx, Mickey Cochrane, Al Simmons, and Lefty Grove, the Athletics were again baseball's top team.

Soon, however, Mack again peddled his best players, once more reducing the A's to mediocrity and eventually ineptitude. Starting in 1934, the Athletics never again came close to league supremacy, finishing in the second division 14 straight seasons, including nine times in last place.

A significant change happened in 1933, when Pennsylvania's blue laws, which since 1794 had prohibited teams and other businesses from operating on Sundays, were amended. The revision allowed most sports to play on the Sabbath between 2:00 p.m. and 7:00 p.m.

Two other developments occurred in the mid-1930s. Already practiced at Baker Bowl, Mack started a Knothole Gang, where youngsters were admitted to games for free. Ladies Day games in which women were admitted for reduced prices were also inaugurated.

In 1935, Mack, unhappy that spectators climbed to the rooftops of houses along Twentieth Street and watched games with the A's receiving no revenue, added 22 feet to the 12-foot-high right-field wall, effectively blocking the view from that spot. Mack was taken to court by homeowners attempting to have the wall, called the "Spite Wall," removed but, represented by future Philadelphia mayor Richardson Dilworth, won the case.

Four years later, Mack again raised the ire of neighborhood residents with a plan to install lights for night baseball. Residents claimed that the crowds, noise, and lights would destroy their peace and quiet. Moreover, they could not sit on their porches at night for fear of being hit by home-run balls. Most disturbing, fans in the right-field upper deck could look into their bedrooms.

Ultimately, the grievances were quelled, and eight 146-foot-high light towers with a candlepower totaling two billion watts were installed at a cost of $115,000. On May 16, 1939, the Athletics defeated Cleveland, 8-3, in the first American League night game.

By the 1930s, Shibe Park had upper decks all the way around the field except from dead center to the right-field line, raising the park's capacity to 33,000. A parking lot was also in operation on the third-base side of the ballpark, while Reyburn Park gave a woodsy touch to the area across Lehigh Avenue. Houses and factories stood behind the Somerset and Twentieth Streets side of the field. (Baseball Hall of Fame and Library.)

The Athletics and Phillies met in a City Series that ran from 1903 through 1954. Some games were played before the season began, others during the season, and a few after the season was over. Nine games—the most ever played—took place in 1928, with the A's winning seven of them. The managers that year were Burt Shotton of the Phillies and Connie Mack, who shook hands before the first game at Shibe Park. (Robert D. Warrington.)

A WHOLE NEW LOOK

The Athletics won their first pennant in 15 years in 1929 and faced the Chicago Cubs in the World Series. From left to right, future Hall of Famers Rogers Hornsby, Hack Wilson, Al Simmons, and Jimmie Foxx all participated. With the last three games played at Shibe Park, the A's won the series four games to one. The fourth game became one of the most famous in World Series history, when the Athletics scored 10 runs in the seventh inning to overcome an 8-0 deficit and win the game, 10-8. Simmons led off the inning with a home run, then later scored the A's ninth run on Jimmy Dykes's two-run double, which also chased home Foxx with the 10th run.

The population of Philadelphia was exploding, and so was the area surrounding Shibe Park. By the third decade of the 20th century, houses, businesses, and factories virtually covered the area. Shibe Park (lower left) was just seven blocks down Lehigh Avenue from Baker Bowl (upper center). Both the Phillies and Athletics had their own fans, many of whom paid little attention to the other. But at least there was usually a game at one ballpark or the other. (Temple University Urban Archives.)

SHIBE PARK–CONNIE MACK STADIUM

With Shibe Park's right-field wall just 12 feet high, sitting on rooftops along Twentieth Street was a popular and cheap way to watch a game. Homeowners charged a nominal fee (usually 35¢) and installed bleachers on the upper roofs. The A's World Series games in 1929, 1930, and 1931 were all popular attractions, and fans jammed Twentieth Street while thousands more watched from roofs and second-floor windows.

Future Hall of Famers catcher Mickey Cochrane (left) and pitcher "Lefty" Grove formed a brilliant battery. Grove was one of baseball's greatest left-handed pitchers, winning 300 games during his career. He pitched nine seasons with the Athletics, including 1931, when he posted a 31-4 record. Cochrane, one of the game's finest catchers, also spent nine years with the A's, his best season coming in 1930, when he hit .357.

Keeping the playing field in good condition is an important duty. This 1930s groundskeeping crew used many tools that are similar to today's implements.

Many memorable home runs were hit at Shibe Park by (from left to right) Lou Gehrig, Jimmie Foxx, and Babe Ruth. Among them, Gehrig smacked three homers and drove in eight runs in a game in 1930 and clouted four homers in one game in 1932. In 1928, Foxx was the first player ever to drill a homer over the left-field roof. Ruth not only slugged his first hit as a New York Yankee at Shibe Park, he also hit his 54th homer there in his record-breaking season in 1920.

In the early days at Shibe Park, almost the entire crowd at a game consisted of male fans, most of them wearing coats, ties, and hats. Especially during big games, fans were packed tightly together on narrow, wooden benches, a condition that discouraged women from attending games.

A WHOLE NEW LOOK

The 1930 World Series pitted the Athletics against the St. Louis Cardinals. The scorecard could be purchased for 25¢, while a ticket for a seat in the upper deck behind home plate cost $5.50.

With the Great Depression in full tilt and both the Athletics and Phillies playing miserably, meager crowds attended games in the 1930s and 1940s. And no wonder, because from 1934 through 1946 the A's finished sixth twice, seventh two times, and eighth nine times. After coming to Shibe Park in 1938, the Phillies through 1946 placed eighth seven times and seventh and fifth each once. Often the crowds at a game totaled about 1,500. The right-field wall at Shibe Park was

In the 1930s, it dawned on the baseball powers that women should be encouraged to attend games. In 1936, Connie Mack inaugurated Ladies Day, offering heavily discounted admission prices to women.

A WHOLE NEW LOOK

heightened to 34 feet in 1935. This increase effectively blocked the views of fans who watched games from the rooftops of houses along Twentieth Street. Homeowners filed a lawsuit to try to block construction of the wall, but the Athletics prevailed. The neighborhood fans nicknamed it the "Spite Wall."

The Ladies Day plan was a success, and for the next two decades, Ladies Day was a popular feature at Shibe Park at Thursday afternoon games.

Despite opposition by residents on Twentieth Street, who took Connie Mack to court but lost, light towers were installed by Westinghouse in 1939. Eight towers holding 780 fifteen-hundred-watt floodlights surrounded the ballpark. Here, the new lights were turned on and tested after their installation. Soon afterward, the first American League night game was played at Shibe Park with the Athletics defeating the Cleveland Indians, 8-3. Only 15,109 showed up for the game. (Robert D. Warrington.)

After Connie Mack broke up another championship run, one of the few stars on the Athletics was Bob Johnson. An outstanding hitter who clobbered more than 30 home runs three times and batted .290 or more eight times in his 10 years with the A's, Johnson played with the team from 1933 to 1942. With some of the worst teams in their history, the Athletics finished in last place six times over that period.

A WHOLE NEW LOOK

The Elephant Room, a combination eating and memorabilia facility, was a fixture at Shibe Park in the 1940s when ex-pitcher Chief Bender (left) stopped for a visit.

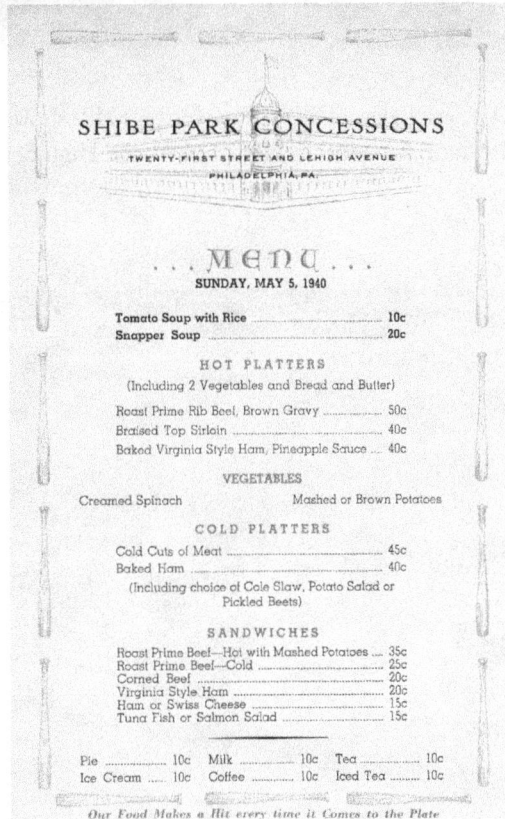

SHIBE PARK CONCESSIONS

TWENTY-FIRST STREET AND LEHIGH AVENUE
PHILADELPHIA, PA.

. . . M E N U . . .
SUNDAY, MAY 5, 1940

Tomato Soup with Rice	10c
Snapper Soup	20c

HOT PLATTERS
(Including 2 Vegetables and Bread and Butter)

Roast Prime Rib Beef, Brown Gravy	50c
Braised Top Sirloin	40c
Baked Virginia Style Ham, Pineapple Sauce	40c

VEGETABLES

Creamed Spinach   Mashed or Brown Potatoes

COLD PLATTERS

Cold Cuts of Meat	45c
Baked Ham	40c

(Including choice of Cole Slaw, Potato Salad or Pickled Beets)

SANDWICHES

Roast Prime Beef—Hot with Mashed Potatoes	35c
Roast Prime Beef—Cold	25c
Corned Beef	20c
Virginia Style Ham	20c
Ham or Swiss Cheese	15c
Tuna Fish or Salmon Salad	15c

Pie	10c	Milk	10c	Tea	10c
Ice Cream	10c	Coffee	10c	Iced Tea	10c

Our Food Makes a Hit every time it Comes to the Plate

Prices at Shibe Park concessions stands were listed on posters that hung on the wall. This 1940 menu lists some pretty good bargains. (Robert D. Warrington.)

An aerial view of Shibe Park in the 1940s shows homes surrounding two sides of the ballpark. Reyburn Park and Dobbins Vocational High School can be seen in the upper left.

On opening day in 1941, the Athletics' starting lineup included (from left to right) catcher Frankie Hayes, first baseman Dick Siebert, second baseman Lawrence "Crash" Davis, shortstop Al Brancato, and third baseman Pete Suder. As Philadelphia teams usually did in that era, the A's finished in last place while losing 100 games.

A WHOLE NEW LOOK

4

THE PHILLIES MOVE IN

Get out of Baker Bowl. Ditch that dump and move to a quality ballpark. Play ball at Shibe Park, where the conditions are excellent and the problems are minimal.

Since the late 1920s, Connie Mack had been making that pitch to Phillies presidents William Baker and then Gerry Nugent, trying to persuade them to escape the decrepit old ballpark seven blocks down Lehigh Avenue and relocate to Shibe Park. Nugent, especially, wanted to accept Mack's invitation but could not escape the lease that kept his team tied to Baker Bowl.

Finally, in 1938, a year in which Dobbins Vocational High School was built across the street, Nugent signed an agreement to rent Shibe Park. The Phillies moved into their new quarters in mid-season and on July 4 made their Shibe Park debut, splitting a doubleheader with the Boston Bees.

The Phillies were not strangers to the ballpark. For 30 years, they had played City Series games there against the Athletics. (The City Series continued until the A's left town holding a 53-48 advantage in games played at Shibe Park.) They also played 12 games there in 1927 when they vacated Baker Bowl because a section of the stands collapsed.

Throughout much of the 1930s and early 1940s, the area surrounding the ballpark was suffering. At the peak of the Great Depression, local factories, banks, and businesses closed, and unemployed people wandered the streets in search of work. A few managed to land part-time jobs at Shibe Park.

In 1943, Shibe Park was the site of the first All-Star Game played at night. Before a crowd of 31,938, the American League captured a 5-3 victory with the help of Bobby Doerr's three-run homer. In 1948, while involved in the pennant race until late August, the A's drew 945,076 for the season, the club's highest attendance in Philadelphia. Another major event took place in 1947, when 41,660 fans (40,952 paid) jammed the park to see the Brooklyn Dodgers' Jackie Robinson make his first appearance in Philadelphia.

The fans always played a major role in events at Shibe Park. Although it was noted for its obstructed views, its delicious hot dogs, and its absence of beer until 1961, Shibe Park was also known for its loud, boisterous, often unruly fans. Most of them rooted for the home team, but regardless of which team the player was on, no one escaped the relentless scrutiny of the fans.

Baker Bowl—originally called Philadelphia Base Ball Park—was opened in 1887 and for the next 51 and a half years was the home of the Phillies. Located at Broad Street and Lehigh Avenue, just seven blocks from Shibe Park's main entrance, it had deteriorated badly by the 1930s and was derisively called a dump.

The Phillies had played in City Series games at Shibe Park and in 12 regular season games there in 1927 after a section of Baker Bowl collapsed. For a decade after, Connie Mack tried to persuade the Phillies to relocate fully to Shibe Park. That effort was finally successful in 1938, when Mack (front right) and Phillies owner Gerry Nugent (front left) sat at a table on July 1 and signed an agreement that provided for the ballpark to be rented to the Phillies. Standing behind them are (from left to right) Judge Harry S. McDevitt, Stephen Newhall, Robert Irwin, Cornelius Haggerty Jr., Connie Mack Jr., Frank McFarland, Douglas Nicholson, Robert Mair, Channing Ellery, and Roy Mack. (Robert D. Warrington.)

THE PHILLIES MOVE IN

On July 4, three days after agreeing to move to Shibe Park, the Phillies made their debut in a doubleheader against the Boston Bees. The Phils lost the opener, 10-5, but came back to win the nightcap, 10-2, with Claude Passeau, who had lost the last game at Baker Bowl, earning the victory.

Taylor Grant (foreground) was an early broadcaster of Phillies games, working in the 1937–1938 and 1941–1942 seasons. Later, he served as a local television newsman before becoming a nationally prominent network newscaster.

After retiring as a player, Babe Ruth, who once hit six home runs in four games at Shibe Park, returned to the stadium in 1938 as the third-base coach with the Brooklyn Dodgers.

Mired in a five-year streak in which they finished last and lost more than 100 games each season, the 1940 Phillies looked anxiously for a rain out. The hopeful group standing in the Phillies dugout at Shibe Park include, from left to right, Emmett Mueller, Morrie Arnovich, Joe Marty, and Gus Suhr.

THE PHILLIES MOVE IN

One of the great Phillies hitters of all time, Chuck Klein (left) was honored in 1940 at Shibe Park after joining the club for the third time. Klein, who began his big-league career in 1928 with the Phillies and who in 1930 while playing at Baker Bowl hit .386 with 40 home runs and 170 RBI, ultimately was inducted into the Hall of Fame. Presenting him with a set of golf clubs and other goodies are manager Hans Lobert and Judge Harry S. McDevitt.

Sometimes in the early 1940s, a Phillies game would draw less than 1,000 fans. In 1940, the Phillies drew just 207,177 fans for the entire season. A sparse crowd was in attendance for this 1942 game when Danny Litwhiler scored for the Phils against the Chicago Cubs. That year, Litwhiler set a major-league record for outfielders by playing in more than 150 games without making an error.

Ted Williams became the last major-leaguer to hit .400 for a season after going 6-for-8 in a doubleheader on the final day of the season. It happened at Shibe Park on September 28, 1941. Williams entered the game with a .39955 batting average. Even though that would be rounded off to .400, Williams insisted on playing, saying, "If I'm going to be a .400 hitter, I want to have more than my toenails on the line." Williams (shown being congratulated by Boston Red Sox manager Joe Cronin) had four hits, including a home run, in five trips to the plate in the first game. He went 2-for-3 in the nightcap, hitting a double that broke an amplifier atop the right-field wall.

Although Phillies crowds at Shibe Park were usually small during a period between 1938 and 1942 when the team lost more than 100 games in five straight seasons, one never knew who would show up. In this case, it was a group of cowboys from Billings, Montana. Members of an Elks club, they were greeted by pitcher Cy Blanton (left) and manager Hans Lobert.

The first major-league player drafted into World War II was Phillies pitcher Hugh Mulcahy in 1941. The following year, the team's printed schedule pictured Mulcahy on the cover.

Connie Mack's 50th year as a big-league manager was celebrated in 1944 at Shibe Park. Participants in the celebration for Mack, who began his career as a skipper in 1894 with the Pittsburgh Pirates, included the living members of Connie's all-time all-star team. The group included, from left to right, Bill Dickey, George Sisler, Frank Baker, Lefty Grove, Honus Wagner, and Walter Johnson.

Military veterans were often saluted at Shibe Park. In this case, Cpl. George Hauser, a patient at Valley Forge Military Hospital, throws out the first ball on opening day in 1946. He is flanked by (from left to right) Boston Braves manager Billy Southworth, Philadelphia mayor Bernard Samuel, and Phillies pilot Ben Chapman.

One of the legendary figures in Philadelphia broadcasting history was By Saam, a Texas native who began his local career in 1939. Saam worked both Phillies and Athletics home games before joining the A's full-time in 1950. After the A's left town, Saam returned to the Phillies in 1955 and handled the play-by-play from a skimpy broadcast booth high above the third-base line until retiring in 1975. In 1990, Saam was inducted into the Baseball Hall of Fame.

THE PHILLIES MOVE IN

Although he never played with a Philadelphia team, Mickey Vernon was one of the area's most popular players. A two-time American League batting champion with the Washington Senators, Vernon was a native of Marcus Hook, Pennsylvania, just south of the city. In 1946, the year of his first batting title, Vernon was honored by his Hook friends at Shibe Park. Sid Stesis, chairman of the honoring committee, is seen greeting Mickey and his wife, Lib, on the special day. (Temple University Urban Archives.)

After the end of World War II, fans flocked back to ballparks around the nation—Shibe Park was no exception. In 1946, the Phillies drew 1,045,247 fans, the largest attendance in team history up to that point. At Sunday doubleheaders like this one, nearly every seat was taken. (Temple University Urban Archives.)

Pulling a roller to smooth the playing surface was once done at Shibe Park by an ancient-looking machine that was driven around the infield and outfield grass. Meanwhile, numbers in the old scoreboard at the ballpark were installed by hand from a narrow runway between the wall and scoreboard.

THE PHILLIES MOVE IN

Sometimes when they wanted privacy, Phillies general manager Herb Pennock (left) and owner Bob Carpenter would find unusual places to discuss business. One place was an upstairs balcony on the third-base side of the ballpark. Instead of soft seats, they sat on soft-drink boxes.

One doubleheader in 1946 drew a record 35,148 spectators. The first game was decided when third baseman Jim Tabor (right) hit a home run in the 10th inning to give the Phils a 5-4 win. Seven years earlier, as a member of the Boston Red Sox, Tabor slammed three home runs, including two grand slams, in the second game of a Fourth of July twin bill at Shibe Park. In one of the greatest batting exhibitions in the ballpark's history, Tabor finished the day with four homers, 11 RBI, and seven runs scored. In 1936, the New York Yankees' Tony Lazzeri collected an American League–record 11 RBI with a triple and three homers, including two grand slams, in a 25-2 victory over the Athletics.

Phillies and Athletics pennants were popular items sold at Shibe Park souvenir stands. The Phillies pennant in the late 1940s depicted a blue jay. Although the team's nickname was never officially changed to Blue Jays, it was used as a secondary name between 1944 and 1948. The A's symbol was the ever-present White Elephant, a name given to the team by John McGraw.

In finishing in fifth place, the 1946 Phillies placed higher than any Phils team since the 1932 club wound up fourth. The 1946 squad included, from left to right, outfielder Ron Northey, shortstop Skeeter Newsome, second baseman Emil Verban, and third baseman Jim Tabor.

The last pitcher to toss a no-hitter for the home team at Shibe Park was the Athletics' Bill McCahan, who did it on September 3, 1947. McCahan, a native Philadelphian, beat the Washington Senators, 3-0. It was one of just 16 big-league wins for the former Duke University star who once played with a pro basketball team called the SPHAS (South Philadelphia Hebrew Association).

Jackie Robinson's first big-league game in Philadelphia was a history-making event that drew 41,660 (40,952 paid) to a May 11, 1947, doubleheader at Shibe Park. No baseball game at the ballpark ever drew a bigger crowd. Robinson had a number of other dramatic occasions at Shibe Park, including a 14th-inning home run that gave the Brooklyn Dodgers a 9-8 victory over the Phillies in the last game of the 1951 season. The win vaulted Brooklyn into a tie for the National League pennant, after which it lost in a special playoff series to Bobby Thomson and the New York Giants.

Hall of Famer Jackie Robinson broke Baseball's color barrier in 1947.

The 1947 doubleheader against the Dodgers resulted in two Phillies wins, with Emil John "Dutch" Leonard (left) winning the opener, 7-3, and Lynwood "Schoolboy" Rowe (right) capturing the nightcap, 5-4. The two veteran hurlers were mainstays of the Phils pitching staff until the "Whiz Kids" moved in.

THE PHILLIES MOVE IN

After being traded to the Phillies early in the 1947 season, Harry Walker etched his name in Philadelphia baseball annals by winning the National League batting championship with a .363 average. Walker lost his center-field job to Richie Ashburn the following year and left the team at the end of the season.

The Athletics' pitching staff in the late 1940s was one of the team's strong points. Joining Connie Mack, key members of the starting rotation included, from left to right, Lou Brissie, Phil Marchildon, and Joe Coleman.

Through most of their years in Philadelphia, the Athletics used a white elephant as their symbol. The burly creature was often displayed on scorecards such as this one in 1948. At other times, Connie Mack commanded a familiar spot on the fronts of scorecards.

By the late 1940s, with both the Phillies and the Athletics playing well, Shibe Park was pulling in big crowds again. The area, with Dobbins Tech (upper left), a Philco plant (upper right), and houses all around, was also bustling with activity. On days when games were played, the area became filled with the sounds of car horns, police whistles, trolley bells, and the voices of vendors and fans, all raising the noise level to unnatural heights.

Sam Chapman, a former All-American running back from the University of California, was the Athletics' big hitter and one of its most popular players in the 1940s. Greeted by Ferris Fain and Elmer Valo (no. 10) as he crossed the plate during a game at Shibe Park, Chapman homered in double figures nine times with the A's.

Bullpen phones were installed at Shibe Park in 1949. Pitching coach Earl Brucker (left) gets a call from Connie Mack as, from left to right, Les McCrabb, Bobby Shantz, and Alex Kellner listen.

THE PHILLIES MOVE IN

One of Shibe Park's most memorable games occurred in 1949, when Phillies batters hit five home runs in one inning in a game against the Cincinnati Reds. From left to right, Schoolboy Rowe, Del Ennis, Andy Seminick, and Willie Jones carried the big sticks in the 12-3 win over the Reds and former Phils pitcher Ken Raffensberger. Seminick hit two homers as the Phils scored 10 runs in the eighth inning.

Andy Seminick arrives at the Phillies dugout after hitting a home run against the St. Louis Cardinals. This 1949 picture is particularly noteworthy because it shows Dave Zinkoff (dark shirt in center) standing alongside the Phillies dugout. At the time, "The Zink," as he was known, was the Phils' public-address announcer. For many years both before and after that, Zink was a nationally prominent PA announcer for the SPHAS, the Harlem Globetrotters, and the Philadelphia Warriors and 76ers.

Official SCORE BOOK

PLAY BALL

10c	**CITY SERIES**	1951

ATHLETICS vs. PHILLIES

SHIBE PARK

The City Series was an extremely popular way for fans to see the Athletics and Phillies square off against each other. In 1951, a program cost just 10¢. Since the series began in 1903, the Phillies won 16, the A's won 22, and there were 10 ties before the event ended in 1954. In 1928, there were nine meetings between the teams, with the A's winning seven.

THE PHILLIES MOVE IN

5

SOMETHING IS
ALWAYS GOING ON

One of the special features of Shibe Park was that there was almost always a game going on. If the Phillies were not playing at home, the Athletics were. And if neither was home, some other teams were probably on the field.

The foremost occupant of those kinds of games was the Philadelphia Eagles. Formed in 1933, the Eagles spent their early years playing mostly at first Baker Bowl, Temple Stadium, and Municipal Stadium. Drawing poorly and losing regularly, the Eagles finally found a more permanent home in 1940 when they moved into Shibe Park. Except for a split season in 1943, they would stay there through the 1957 season, compiling an overall 58-35-6 record. The Eagles' biggest single-game crowd came in 1946, when 40,059 packed the house in a game against the New York Giants.

During their 17 seasons at Twenty-first Street and Lehigh Avenue, the Eagles had 11 winning seasons. In what was the brightest era in club history, the Birds went to the NFL championship game three straight times between 1947 and 1949, winning the title in 1948 and 1949.

The 1948 championship battle that pitted the Eagles against the Chicago Cardinals was one of the two greatest games (the other was the 1960 championship game) in Eagles history. With more than one foot of snow sitting atop one ton of hay that covered the field, players from both sides helped shovel off the field before the game. The contest was held in a blinding snowstorm, with Steve Van Buren's touchdown giving the Eagles a 7-0 victory.

Many other notable football games were played at Shibe Park, including an NFL championship game in 1926 in which the Frankford Yellow Jackets defeated the Chicago Bears, 7-6. One year earlier, the NFL's Pottsville Maroons downed a team of Notre Dame University alumni, including the Four Horsemen, 9-6.

Villanova University also played football at Shibe Park in the 1940s, and in the 1930s, Howard and Lincoln Universities played their annual Thanksgiving game there.

Negro-league baseball was also on display at Shibe Park. The Hilldale Daises and later the Philadelphia Stars played there, especially on Mondays when there was no big-league contest. In two games played there in 1920, a team of all-stars put together by Babe Ruth lost to the Atlantic City Bacharachs, then came back later to beat the Hilldale Daisies. In 1923, Hilldale, a club from Darby, defeated the American Giants of Chicago three games to one for the Negro National League championship.

In 1924, the Daisies met the Kansas City Monarchs at Shibe Park in the first two games of the first Negro League World Series, with each team winning one game.

In another noteworthy game in 1934, an all-white team led by St. Louis Cardinals pitching great Dizzy Dean and his brother Paul lost a doubleheader to the newly crowned Negro National League champion Philadelphia Stars.

Boxing was also a major part of the Shibe Park scenario. Starting in 1914, when the first fight pitted Jack O'Brien and Bob Fitzsimmons, more than 50 cards were held on the diamond with crowds of usually 15,000 or more in attendance. Benny Leonard (1917), Benny Bass (1927), Lou Salica (1941), Bob Montgomery (1946), and Ike Williams (1948) all won titles there. And fighters ranging from Tommy Loughran, Lew Tendler, Kid Chocolate, and Sugar Ray Robinson to Beau Jack, Joey Giardello, Gil Turner, Joe Walcott, Ezzard Charles, and Harold Johnson all staged major bouts at the ballpark before the last fight was held there in 1958.

Softball wizard Eddie Feigner of "The King and His Court" fame played at Shibe Park; Max Patkin, "The Clown Prince of Baseball," entertained there; and Philadelphia Public and Catholic League baseball and football teams often took the field. The park also played host to wrestling matches and soccer games.

Standing president Herbert Hoover saw a World Series game at Shibe Park, and Franklin D. Roosevelt campaigned there. Presidential candidates Wendall Wilkie, Henry Wallace, and Richard Nixon also campaigned there. And circuses, religious rallies, and jazz concerts were among the many other kinds of events staged over the years at Shibe Park.

The football field at Shibe Park extended from the first-base line to left field. With 6,000 temporary seats added in right field, the ballpark had a capacity of 39,000 for football. The Eagles' rent was 15 percent of their gate receipts. (Temple University Urban Archives.)

SOMETHING IS ALWAYS GOING ON

Two stars of the Eagles' NFL Eastern Division championship in 1947 were tackle and captain Al Wistert (left) and running back Steve Van Buren. Earle "Greasy" Neale (right) was the head coach. Ironically, Neale, who became the greatest coach in Eagles history and a member of the Pro Football Hall of Fame, played as an outfielder with the Phillies in 1921.

Part of the gridiron ran across the baseball infield. In this play, the Eagles' Neil Armstrong is being knocked down near second base by John Cochran of the Chicago Cardinals in a game in 1947.

Temporary bleachers were installed in front of the right-field wall for football games at Shibe Park. Fans sitting in the grandstands down the right-field line were a long way from the action. (Jim Gallagher.)

Quarterback Davey O'Brien (no. 8) was a Heisman Trophy winner and a first-round draft pick of the Eagles in 1939. He played only two seasons with the Eagles, once throwing a record 60 passes in a game. O'Brien quit the Eagles to join the FBI, and in his final game in 1940, owner and team president Bert Bell presented him with a silver platter.

SOMETHING IS ALWAYS GOING ON

One of the greatest games in Eagles history occurred in 1948 at Shibe Park, when the Birds defeated the Chicago Cardinals 7-0 to win their first NFL championship in near-blizzard conditions. Nearly one foot of snow covered the field before the game, but both teams elected to play. Some 28,864 fans came to the ballpark to watch the action. Steve Van Buren (no. 15) plowed into the end zone from the five-yard line to score the only touchdown. Thinking the game would not be played in a blinding snowstorm, Van Buren remained at home in Lansdowne. Finally, deciding he should better go to the ballpark, the Eagles' great running back rode public transportation before walking the final seven blocks down Lehigh Avenue to Shibe Park. He arrived just 15 minutes before game time.

For those sitting on the bench during the 1948 championship game, conditions were not exactly ideal. Long coats with large collars helped to keep the players a little bit warmer. (Jim Gallagher.)

Instead of using the playing field at Shibe Park, the Eagles often practiced across the street at what was then called Funfield Recreation Center, which bordered on Reyburn Park. In a workout in 1949, quarterback Tommy Thompson gets set to hand off to Jack Myers (without hood), while Jim Parmer (with hood) takes up a position as a blocker and Steve Van Buren (right) heads off to his left.

In the early
1950s, the Eagles
often drew small
crowds to games
at Shibe Park.
Few were there
to watch as Birds
back Al Pollard
runs toward the
New York Giants'
Bob Hudson in
a game in 1951.

At Shibe Park, players sat on benches close to the stands. While there, (from left to right) Johnny Magee, Jim Parmer, Jay MacDowell, Walt Stickel, Bill Mackrides, and Toy Ledbetter were almost part of the crowd. (Jim Gallagher.)

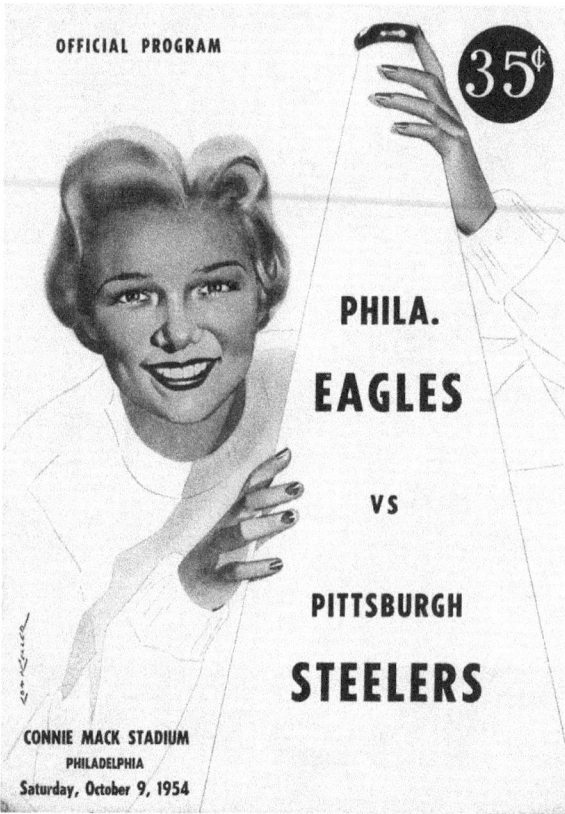

OFFICIAL PROGRAM

35¢

PHILA.

EAGLES

VS

PITTSBURGH

STEELERS

CONNIE MACK STADIUM
PHILADELPHIA
Saturday, October 9, 1954

A program and ticket stub from
a 1954 Eagles–Pittsburgh Steelers
game at Connie Mack Stadium
ably demonstrates how far prices at
sporting events have skyrocketed.
At that game, a lower-deck seat
behind the end zone cost $2,
and a program went for 35¢.

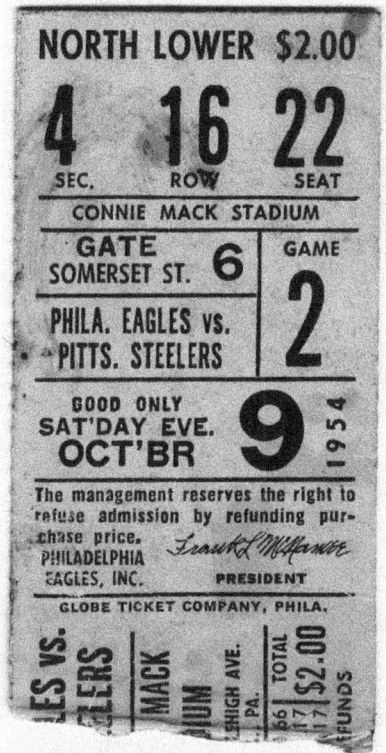

NORTH LOWER $2.00

4   16   22

SEC.   ROW   SEAT

CONNIE MACK STADIUM

GATE
SOMERSET ST. 6   GAME

PHILA. EAGLES vs.
PITTS. STEELERS   2

GOOD ONLY
SAT'DAY EVE.
OCT'BR 9   1954

The management reserves the right to
refuse admission by refunding purchase price.
PHILADELPHIA
EAGLES, INC.   PRESIDENT

GLOBE TICKET COMPANY, PHILA.

SOMETHING IS ALWAYS GOING ON

Before he became a major-league pitcher, Satchel Paige fired some memorable games at Shibe Park. In 1943, while pitching for the Kansas City Monarchs, he hurled in an exhibition game against the Philadelphia Stars. A crowd of 24,165—the largest ever to see an African American baseball game in Philadelphia—showed up. The deciding game of the 1942 Negro League World Series was also held at Shibe Park, with Paige hurling the Monarchs to a 9-5 win over the Homestead Grays.

The Philadelphia Stars (part-owner and manager Ed Bolden in suit) often played at Shibe Park, usually drawing between 10,000 and 12,000 per game. The Stars of the 1940s featured many all-star players and often played as many as 20 games each season at Shibe Park. Players dressed in the Athletics' clubhouse behind the third-base dugout. (William Cash/Lloyd Thompson Baseball Collections, courtesy of the African American Museum of Philadelphia.)

In front of a cheering throng, Franklin D. Roosevelt attended a campaign rally at Shibe Park in 1944 while running for his fourth term as president. Because of his immobility, Roosevelt spoke from inside the limousine that carried him around the field. The only other standing president to appear at Shibe Park was Herbert Hoover, who attended World Series games there in 1929, 1930, and 1931. (Above, Temple University Urban Archives.)

SOMETHING IS ALWAYS GOING ON

During World War II, Shibe Park was the site of numerous military parades and bond drives. A large crowd stood to watch as some military equipment was demonstrated in a special event before a game in 1943.

Local boxers often appeared at Shibe Park during more than 50 fight cards at the ballpark. Jimmy Tygh of Nicetown (left) engaged in a noteworthy preliminary bout with Honey Melodie of Boston in 1940. The 138-pound Tygh battled to a draw in 10 rounds. (Chuck Hasson.)

Bob Montgomery (left) and Harold Johnson (below) were among many Philadelphia boxers who fought at Shibe Park. Montgomery, a two-time lightweight champion, often fought at the ballpark, including in a title fight in 1946 when he knocked out Wesley Mouzon. As a light heavyweight contender, Johnson fought heavyweight contender Ezzard Charles in a major bout in 1953 at Shibe Park. Johnson, who would later become the light heavyweight champ, defeated Charles in a 10-round match.

SOMETHING IS ALWAYS GOING ON

Professional wrestling matches were sometimes held at Shibe Park, including this 1945 bout between Jack Smith and Jim Atlas.

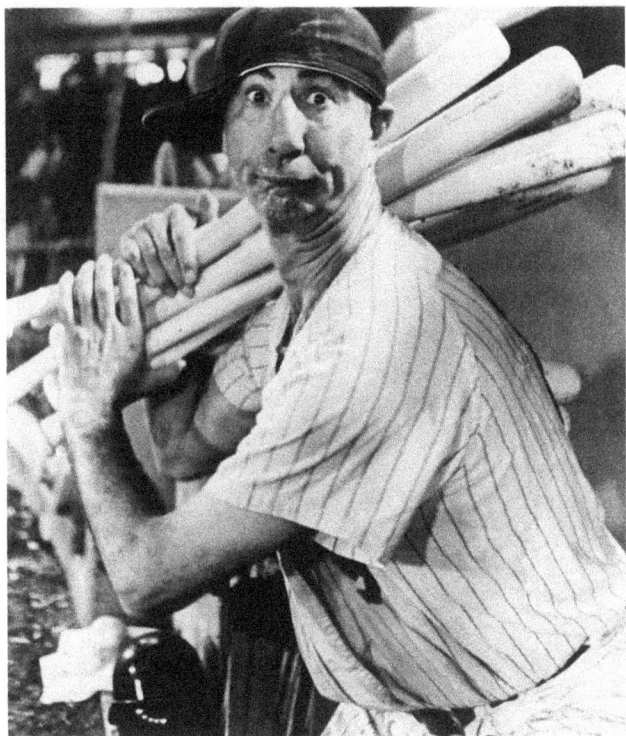

Max Patkin, known as "The Clown Prince of Baseball," did his comic routine a number of times in the 1940s at Shibe Park. A native Philadelphian, Patkin performed at major- and minor-league ballparks throughout the country during a 35-year career in which he once appeared in 3,000 straight games without a miss.

The Greater Kensington String Band was one of many musical groups that performed before games at the ballpark in the 1950s and 1960s. (Bill White.)

In its final years, Shibe Park, by then called Connie Mack Stadium, was the site of frequent concerts. Jazz concerts were especially popular, such as the one in 1959 that featured Count Basie (left) and his band and singer Mahalia Jackson. (Robert D. Warrington.)

SOMETHING IS ALWAYS GOING ON

6

The Year of
the Whiz Kids

In the long history of Shibe Park, no decade was more tumultuous than the 1950s. It was a period in which some momentous shifts occurred that were destined to change forever the face of major-league baseball in Philadelphia.

On the field, the Athletics, except for one flourish in 1948, were not very good. That was reflected in their attendance, which in 1950 dropped to a then-record low of 310,000 for the season.

The A's were no longer Philadelphia's most popular team; there was a new favorite. Although still called the Phillies, it was a vastly different club than the one that had scraped the bottom of the National League for more than 30 years. These Phillies were exciting, and because of their wealth of talented young players they were called "The Whiz Kids." In 1950, they won the team's first pennant since 1915 and went to Philadelphia's first World Series since 1931.

The Phillies had been climbing back to respectability since Bob Carpenter and his family bought the team for $400,000 in 1943. As they did, the crowds increased, ultimately reaching a then-team record 1,217,035 in 1950.

The Whiz Kids were led by future Hall of Famers pitcher Robin Roberts and center fielder Richie Ashburn, Philadelphia native Del Ennis, and some other young players including Willie Jones, Granny Hamner, and Curt Simmons. Veterans Dick Sisler, Andy Seminick, and Eddie Waitkus also contributed heavily to the team managed by Eddie Sawyer.

Many important games were played at Shibe Park, including a July 25 doubleheader in which Bubba Church and Roberts each beat the Chicago Cubs to send the Phils into first place. The Phillies also defeated the Cincinnati Reds, 8-7, in a 19-inning game. After a September slump, the Phillies finally won the pennant on Sisler's three-run homer on the last day of the season at Brooklyn's Ebbets Field.

Shibe Park was the site of the first two World Series games, with the Phils facing the New York Yankees. In the opener, the Whiz Kids lost, 1-0, with reliever Jim Konstanty making a surprise start. Roberts hurled the second game but lost, 2-1, as Joe DiMaggio homered in the 10th inning. Shortly afterward, the Phils lost the series at Yankee Stadium.

Nevertheless, the Whiz Kids had carved a spot in Philadelphia baseball history. And the old ballpark would never again be the site of such a celebrated season.

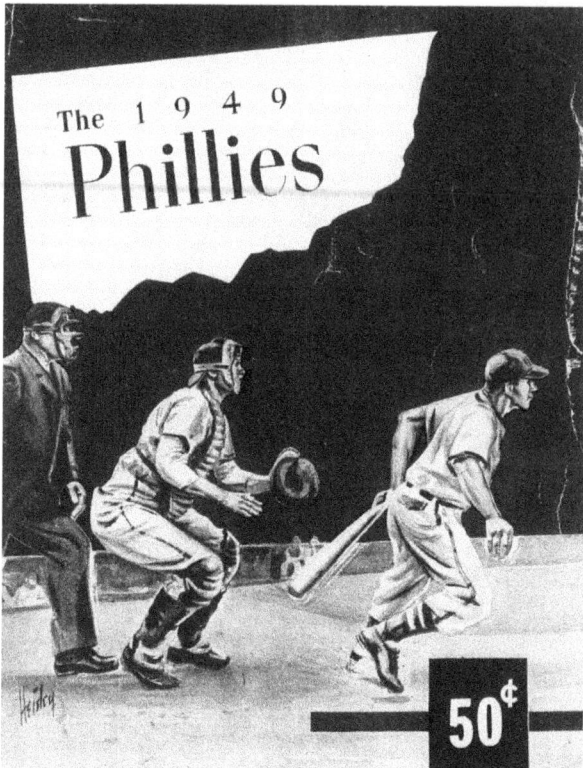

Both the Phillies and Athletics produced their first yearbooks in 1949—they only cost 50¢ apiece.

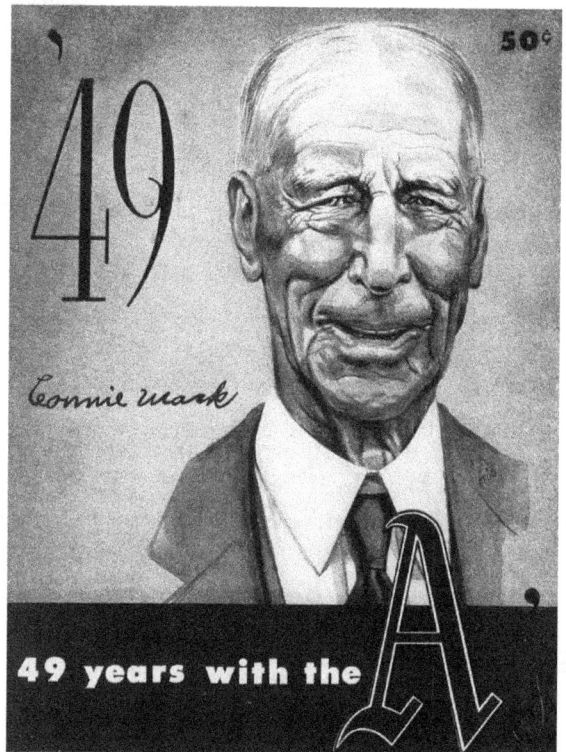

Del Ennis was one of the top Phillies players from 1946, when he was National League Rookie of the Year, through 1956. He was in double figures each year in home runs and drove in more than 100 runs in 6 of his 11 seasons as a Phillie. Having grown up in the Olney section of Philadelphia, Ennis was one of the best local players of all time. This home-run journey ended with a handshake from batboy Kenny Bush, another local who worked for the Phillies for more than 40 years, winding up his career as clubhouse and equipment manager.

Shibe Park groundskeepers had a big job in 1949 cleaning up after fans threw cans, bottles, and other debris on the field following a call in which umpire George Barr ruled that Richie Ashburn had trapped a drive by the New York Giants' Joe Lafata. The Phillies vehemently argued the call, while fans kept littering the field for the next 15 minutes. When they would not stop, the game was forfeited to the Giants. From that game on, all beverages were served at Shibe Park in paper cups.

During the Phillies' pennant-winning season in 1950, bandleader Elliot Lawrence composed a song entitled, "The Fightin' Phils." The song made its debut at Shibe Park with, from left to right, Granny Hamner, Richie Ashburn, Willie Jones, and Dick Sisler joining Lawrence in a pre-game rendition.

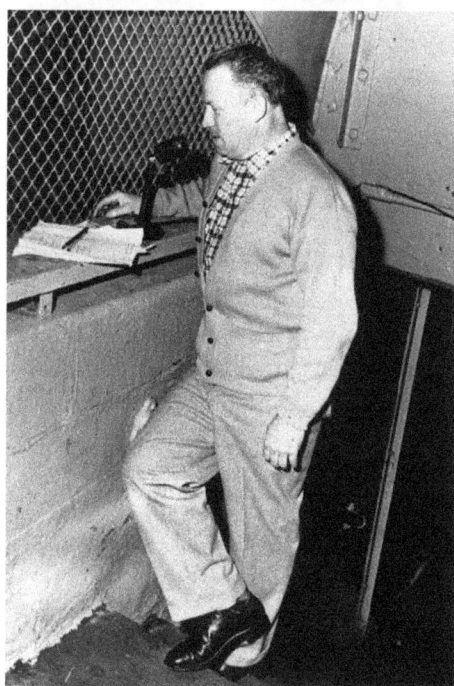

Pete Byron served for many years as the public-address announcer at Shibe Park for both the Phillies and Athletics. He stood in a small enclosed space alongside the home-team dugout.

THE YEAR OF THE WHIZ KIDS

One of the Phillies' greatest pitchers of all time and the ace of the 1950s pitching staff was Robin Roberts, who from 1950 through 1955 won at least 20 games each season. Roberts, who was the winning pitcher in the 1950 pennant-clincher, posted a 28-7 record in 1952. He once pitched 28 straight complete games. Even baseball's winningest pitcher, Cy Young, had to be impressed with that when the two Hall of Famers compared grips.

The Phillies had a new play-by-play announcer in 1950. His name was Gene Kelly, and he quickly became a highly popular broadcaster. Kelly, who stayed with the Phils through the 1959 season, is seen here spending some airtime with, from left to right, Willie Jones, Granny Hamner, Dick Sisler, and Del Ennis.

En route to the National League pennant, the 1950 Phillies pose for a team picture at Shibe Park. Photographers from Philadelphia's three daily newspapers are among those focusing their cameras on the group.

THE YEAR OF THE WHIZ KIDS

Phillies fans, holding a picture of pitcher Jim Konstanty, held a pep rally the night before the World Series opener at Twenty-third Street and Indiana Avenue, just a few blocks from Shibe Park.

Getting there early so they could be the first in line to buy tickets for seats in the bleachers, fans arrived at Shibe Park the night before the opening game of the 1950 World Series. They camped along Somerset Street.

SHIBE PARK–CONNIE MACK STADIUM　　　　　　　　　　　　83

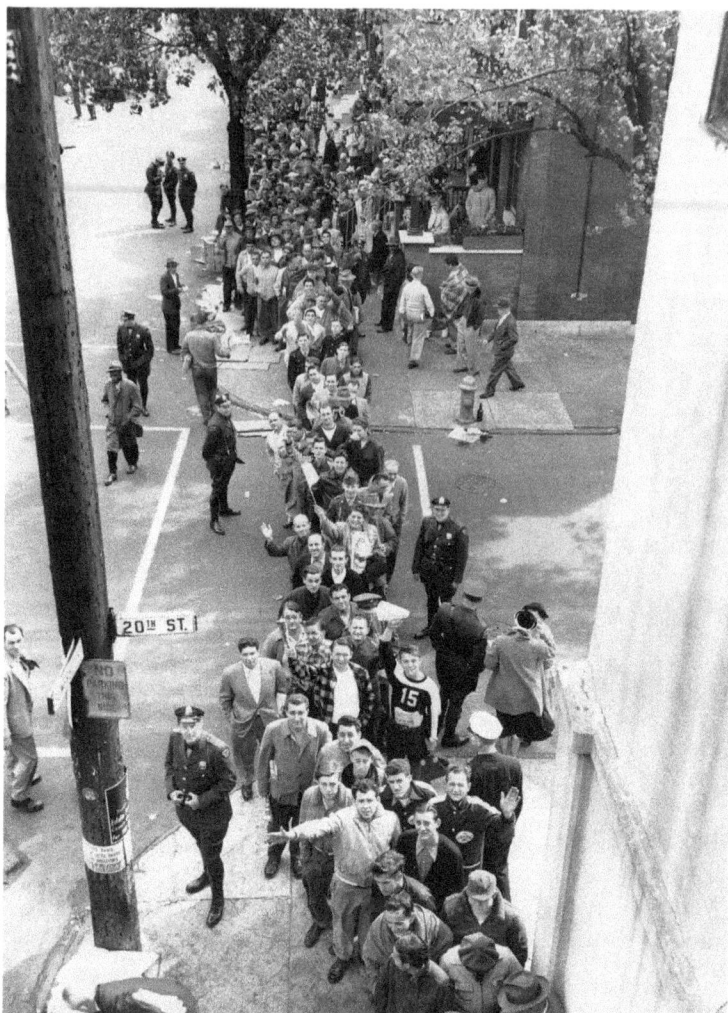

Starting at 7:00 a.m., fans began forming a long line along Somerset Street in hopes of buying bleacher seats for the series opener. By noon, when the ticket windows finally opened, the line was five blocks long.

A ticket for a seat in the upper deck in left-center field for the first game of the 1950 World Series cost just $1.

THE YEAR OF THE WHIZ KIDS

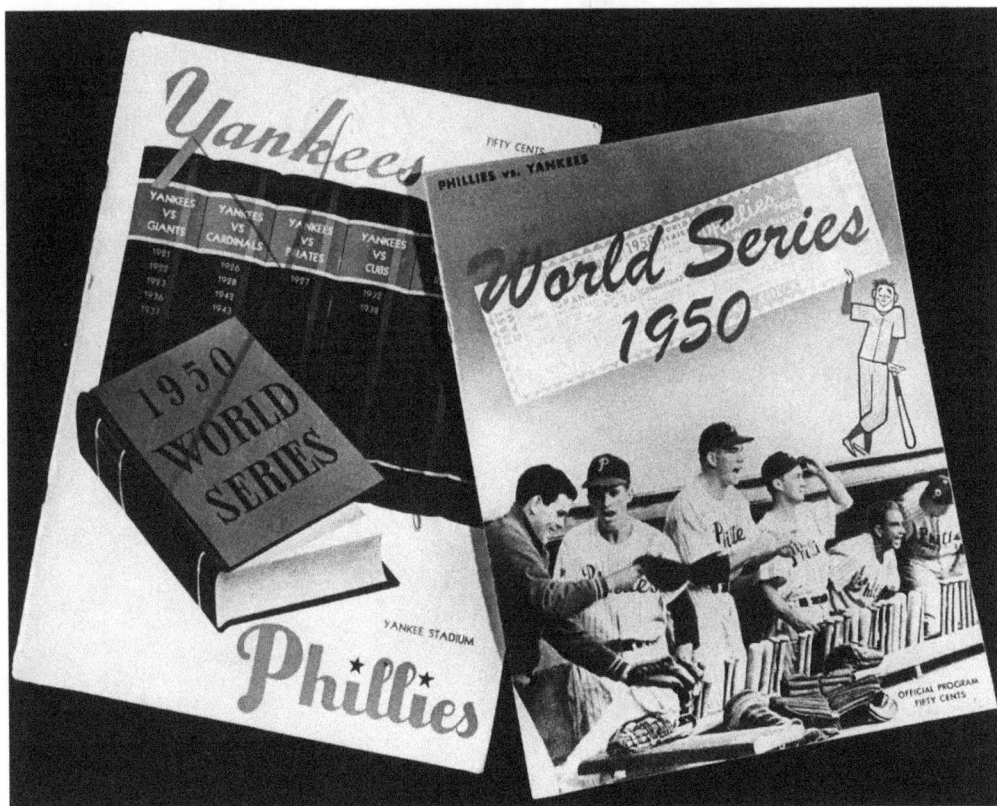

A program for the first World Series game in 1950 showed the Phillies celebrating Dick Sisler's pennant-winning 10th-inning home run in the last game of the season against the Brooklyn Dodgers. The cost of the program was 50¢.

The New York Yankees on the first-base line, the Phillies on the third-base side, and the four umpires stand during the National Anthem before the start of the first series game in 1950.

With a crowd of 30,746 in the stands, the Phillies took the field for the series opener. More than 2,000 seats were empty due to a mix-up in the distribution of tickets. It was the first World Series game played at Shibe Park since 1931.

THE YEAR OF THE WHIZ KIDS

Although he had not started a game since 1948, reliever Jim Konstanty opened the first game for the Phillies. Konstanty, who would go on to be named the National League's Most Valuable Player that year, gave up just four hits in eight innings before being lifted for a pinch-hitter. Konstanty listened to the final inning on a radio in the Phils' clubhouse. The run he surrendered in the fourth inning was the difference, as the Yankees won, 1-0.

Legions of Phillies fans watched the World Series on a giant television screen located downtown outside of Philadelphia City Hall. They saw the Phillies lose both home games while getting swept in four outings.

Shibe Park was filled to capacity for the second game of the World Series with a paid attendance of 32,660, plus several thousand freebies. (Temple University Urban Archives.)

Banners and flags decorated Shibe Park as a capacity crowd watched Robin Roberts face the Yankees in the top of the first inning of the second game.

THE YEAR OF THE WHIZ KIDS

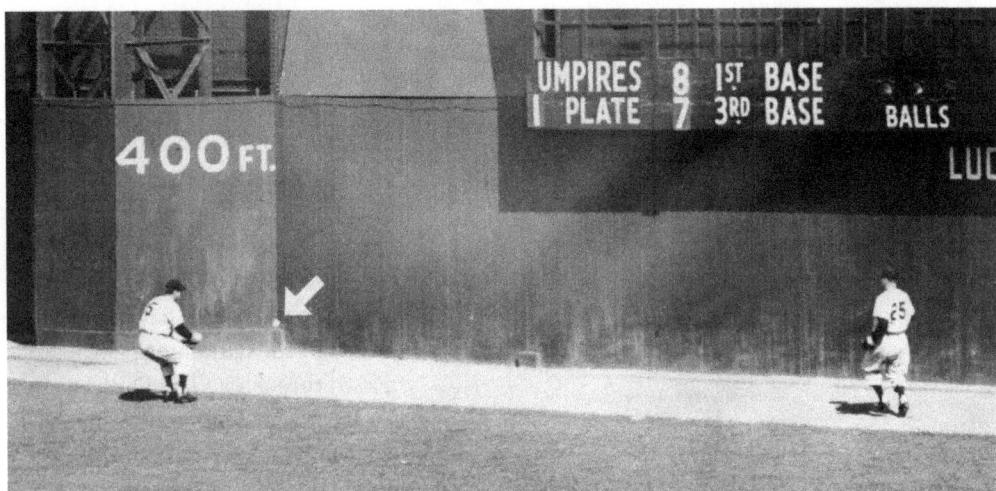

Joe DiMaggio was a key figure in the second game of the World Series. Here he fields a ball that was hit off the wall in deep center field by Granny Hamner that went for a triple. DiMaggio's 10th-inning home run gave the Yankees a 2-1 win.

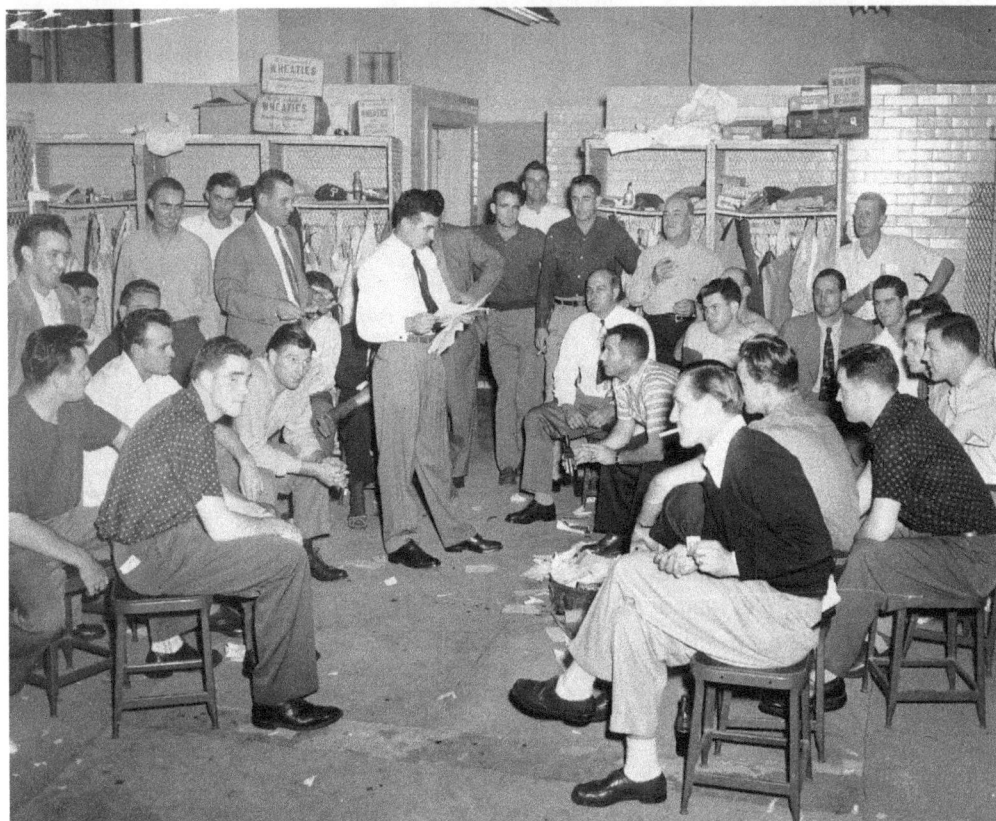

Following the World Series, the 1950 Whiz Kids met in their Shibe Park clubhouse to vote on players' shares. Captain Granny Hamner conducted the meeting, which included players, coaches, and manager Eddie Sawyer (in the center right, in white shirt and tie.)

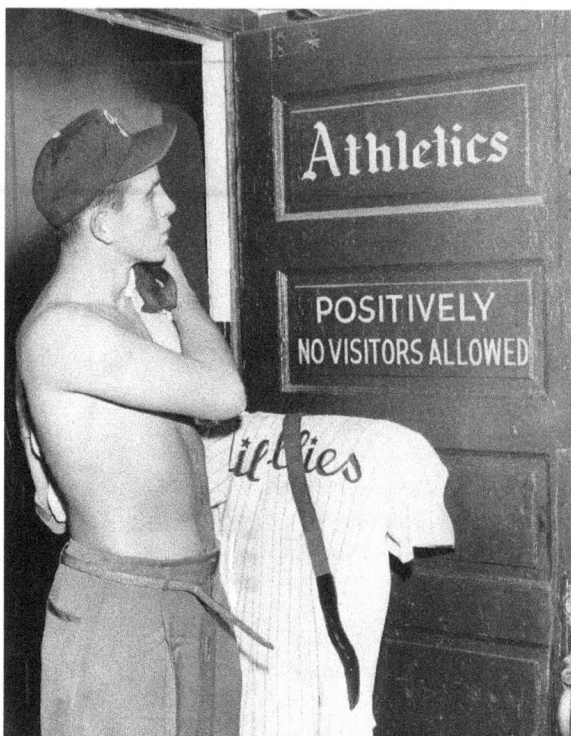

While the Athletics played in Philadelphia, they had their own clubhouse. It was located under the stands and behind the home-team dugout along the third-base line. Players walked from the clubhouse, across a hallway, down a ramp, and into the dugout. If security was lax that day, fans often milled in the hallway as players passed through it. The Phillies had their own clubhouse, a much smaller area, farther down the third-base line. During the 1950 World Series, the plumbing system in the Phils' clubhouse broke, and the team had to move temporarily into the A's locker room. Pitcher Russ Meyer enters half dressed. After the A's left town, the Phillies took over their clubhouse.

A fixture with the Phillies from 1948 until the mid-1960s was trainer Frank Weichec. The first of the club's modern-day trainers, Weichec brought new methods to the art of treating players' injuries while working in a pair of rooms that stood above the back of the locker room and were accessed by climbing a small stairway. The equipment in the trainer's room included a message table, whirlpool bath, heating pads, and diathermic and sonic machines, which were used to treat torn muscles and other ailments.

THE YEAR OF THE WHIZ KIDS

7

FAREWELL TO
THE ATHLETICS

It had been a downhill slide for the Athletics since Connie Mack starting breaking up the team following three straight trips to the World Series between 1929 and 1931. From 1934 through 1950, the A's finished first only once and in last place 10 times.

The slide was reflected in the small crowds attending Athletics home games. The one big shift in that pattern occurred in 1948, when the A's made a run for the pennant before finishing in fourth place. In a doubleheader on July 16 that year, the A's, at the time in first place, met the Cleveland Indians at Shibe Park before a club record 37,684, but they lost both games and got knocked out of first.

Two years later, 87-year-old Connie Mack, with his health fading, gave up the manager's seat that he had held since 1901. Then, in 1954, Mack and his sons Roy and Earle, heavily in debt with no signs of relief, sold the team for $3.5 million to a group led by Arnold Johnson that moved it to Kansas City. In their last game in Philadelphia, played on September 19, 1954, the A's bowed to the New York Yankees, 4-2, with just 1,715 people in the stands.

By then, another shift had happened. On February 13, 1953, Shibe Park was renamed Connie Mack Stadium. Later, Phillies owner Bob Carpenter, who had been paying rent of $125,000 per year, purchased the ballpark for $1,657,000.

In 1955, the center-field fence was moved in from 468 to 447 feet from home plate. The following year, a 50-foot-high scoreboard previously used in Yankee Stadium was purchased for $175,000. It was dismantled and trucked to Philadelphia, where it stood for the rest of the ballpark's existence.

The area surrounding the ballpark was changing, too. In the 1950s, the composition of the neighborhood changed, with the ethnic enclaves of the past replaced by African Americans. Many fans now drove to the ballpark instead of riding public transportation, and parking was at a premium. A 500-car lot across Twenty-first Street was far too small, even after it was increased to a capacity of 850. A group calling itself "The Big Seven" parked cars around the neighborhood. Many fans parked on the streets, where they usually had to pay 25¢ to local kids for "watching your car." Those who did not pay often found their cars with flat tires after returning from a ball game.

Connie Mack's 50 years with the Athletics were recognized with a big Golden Anniversary celebration at Shibe Park in 1950. Players from both the A's and the visiting Boston Red Sox participated. In the two weeks preceding the event, fans signed scrolls (below) placed in the courtyard at Philadelphia City Hall. Mayor Bernard Samuel (to the left of the plaid-shirted boy) was the first signer.

From 1947 through 1951, one of the finest infields in the big leagues consisted of, from left to right, the Athletics' Ferris Fain, Pete Suder, Eddie Joost, and Hank Majeski. The foursome led the American League in double plays three times during that period, setting a major-league record in 1949 with 217. Fain also won the AL batting title in 1951 and 1952.

The last big slugger for the Athletics before they moved out of Philadelphia was left fielder Gus Zernial. The left-field stands were a frequent landing place for Zernial's blasts. He led the league in home runs in 1951 with 33, edging Ted Williams by three.

Yearbooks, scorecards, stickers,
and ticket stubs were popular items
produced by the Phillies and Athletics
during the 1950s and 1960s.

FAREWELL TO THE ATHLETICS

PHILADELPHIA NATIONAL LEAGUE CLUB

CONNIE MACK
STADIUM

1961

ADMIT ONE

THE PHILLIES CORDIALLY INVITE YOU TO BE A GUEST AT CONNIE MACK
STADIUM AND ENJOY A NATIONAL LEAGUE BASEBALL GAME

GOOD ONLY ON AUGUST 7 to OCT. 1

Void if Changed or Mutilated

Present This Pass at the Tax Window, 21st Above Lehigh Ave.,
and Purchase an Admission Ticket.

Good for Special Pass Holder Section Only

| SERVICE CHARGE | 48c | TOTAL |
| CITY TAX | 02c | 50c |

President.

This pass is issued subject to the conditions set forth on the back hereof.

0266

The copy written on both the ticket stub and yearbook was just a bit different than what baseball fans see today. So were the prices. A general-admission ticket in 1961 cost 50¢, while a yearbook in 1966 went for $1.

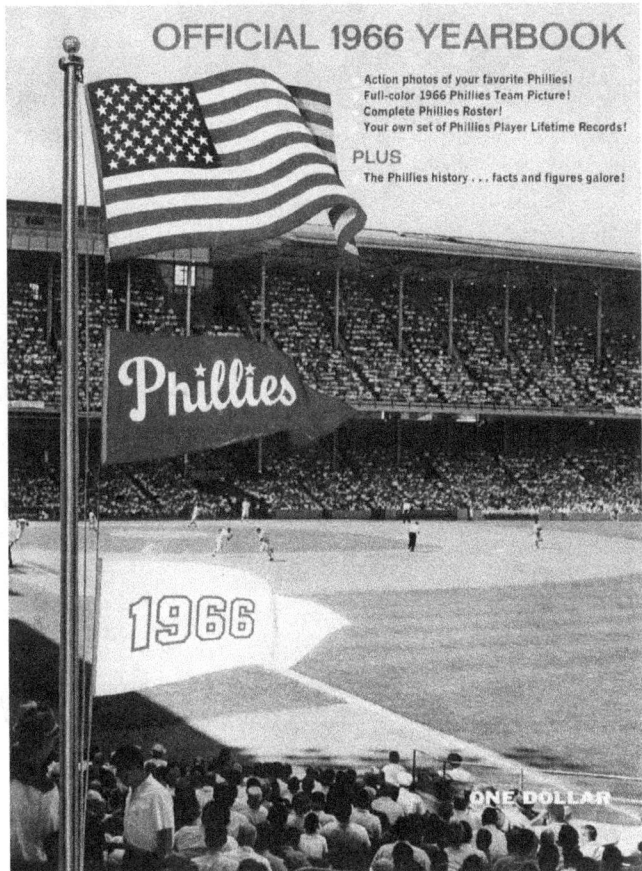

OFFICIAL 1966 YEARBOOK

Action photos of your favorite Phillies!
Full-color 1966 Phillies Team Picture!
Complete Phillies Roster!
Your own set of Phillies Player Lifetime Records!

PLUS

The Phillies history . . . facts and figures galore!

Phillies

1966

ONE DOLLAR

In their last good year before they left town, the Athletics attracted big crowds to Shibe Park in 1952. This was the way it looked outside the main gate at Twenty-first Street and Lehigh Avenue before an A's game against the Boston Red Sox. The A's finished that year in fourth place.

When it rained heavily, dugouts at Shibe Park occasionally became flooded. Such was the case when batboys Vic (left) and Joe Iannucci had to swim their ways out of the dugout in 1952.

96   FAREWELL TO THE ATHLETICS

In its later years, Shibe Park was seldom without organ music. Dorothy Parker Langdon was a popular player in the 1950s. Later, Paul Richardson played the organ at Connie Mack Stadium and at Veterans Stadium. (At right, Temple University Urban Archives.)

The second and last All-Star Game to be held at Shibe Park took place in 1952. In the only All-Star Game ever halted by rain, the National League defeated the American League, 3-2, in five innings with Hank Sauer's two-run homer getting the win. The Phillies' Curt Simmons was the National League's starting pitcher. In the fifth inning, Bobby Shantz of the Athletics struck out Whitey Lockman, Jackie Robinson, and Stan Musial in order. After the game, (from left to right) the National League's Murry Dickson, Chuck Dressen, Pee Wee Reese, Enos Slaughter, Simmons, and Robin Roberts celebrate with league president Warren Giles.

It was a banner season in 1952 for A's pitcher Bobby Shantz. The little lefthander's 24-7 record was the best of his career, and at the end of the season, he was voted Most Valuable Player in the American League. Shantz pitched for 16 years in the big leagues, ending his career in 1964 with the Phillies.

A major alteration took place at Shibe Park on February 13, 1953, when the name of the ballpark was changed to Connie Mack Stadium. Mack had resisted the name change for many years, but while he was in failing health and vacationing in Florida, the Athletics' board of directors voted to make the switch. A small sign on the main entrance noted the change. Especially on warm summer weekend days later in the 1950s, large crowds flocked to the ballpark to watch the Phillies play.

Homes, businesses, and churches lined Lehigh Avenue starting at Twenty-second Street and going up to Twenty-ninth. Trolley-car tracks also were in evidence in the middle of the street. (Temple University Urban Archives.)

SHIBE PARK–CONNIE MACK STADIUM

Since 1900, the only Phillies player to win two batting championships was Richie Ashburn, who was awarded a Silver Bat by National League president Warren Giles after winning his first title in 1955. Ashburn, a future Hall of Famer and a longtime Phils broadcaster after his playing career was over, also won the 1958 batting crown, the last Phillies player to win that title. A brilliant fielder, too, Ashburn ranks as one of the Phillies' greatest position players.

Walls were painted, signs were hung, and the playing surface was prepared as Shibe Park was readied for opening day in 1955. The old scoreboard in right-center field would soon be replaced.

The last big hitting star of the Philadelphia Athletics was first baseman Ferris Fain, affectionately known as "Burrhead." Fain won American League batting championships in both 1951 and 1952 with .334 and .327 averages, respectively. Only one other player in Philadelphia baseball history (Al Simmons in 1930–1931) won back-to-back batting titles.

"Have a seat young man" is something the catcher might have said to the batter in this unusual picture taken at Shibe Park in the late 1940s. What really happened, though, is that Athletics hitter Nellie Fox had to hit the ground after a brushback pitch—he landed seat first. Fox played in parts of three seasons with the Athletics before a senseless trade (for catcher Joe Tipton) sent him to the Chicago White Sox, where he went on to a Hall of Fame career.

Throughout much of the 1950s, the Phillies drew substantial crowds to the ballpark, and people had to endure long lines to get tickets such as this one. The Phillies drew more than one million fans for the first time in 1946. They passed that mark again in 1950 and 1957 before setting a club record with 1,425,891 in 1964.

Taking care of the pitching mound was one of the top priorities for Phillies groundskeepers, including head groundskeeper Ted Forr (left) and Marc O'Donnell. Their techniques do not vary a whole lot from those used today.

The last major change at Connie Mack Stadium came in 1956, when a new scoreboard replaced the antiquated one that had been at the ballpark since 1941. The scoreboard had been at Yankee Stadium before the Phillies bought it for $175,000, dismantled it, and trucked it to Philadelphia. Located in right-center field, it stood 50 feet high. Atop that was a Ballantine beer sign that reached another 10 feet up. Extending another 15 feet high was a Longines watch sign and clock, bringing the entire facility to 75 feet above the playing surface.

A 1957 Phillies game at Connie Mack Stadium attracted a standing-room-only crowd of 37,667. The increased capacity was partly due to the addition of 24 boxes along the playing field; each box had six seats. Because of this addition, dugouts were moved closer to the playing field.

FAREWELL TO THE ATHLETICS

8

THE END OF AN ICON

Although it had been a favorite place of players and fans, Connie Mack Stadium was not destined to go on forever. Not with its rundown condition and obsolescence. Not with the surrounding neighborhood becoming increasingly dangerous. Not with an influx of modern venues appearing throughout the country. By the 1960s, the old ballpark was ready to go.

The stadium, which had been purchased by real estate developer and new Eagles owner Jerry Wolman in 1964 for $600,000, did not die gracefully. The end came into view in 1964, when the Phillies staged a horrific collapse. Afterward, the Phils rarely exceeded mediocrity, and attendance dropped substantially.

It did not help that the area had turned ominous. What was once a friendly, safe neighborhood had changed. The businesses and working-class people had fled. They were replaced by residents much lower on the economic scale.

Crime was a major problem. Robberies and other felonies were common. Frequent crimes were committed inside the ballpark. People were robbed in bathrooms. Women had their pocketbooks snatched. Fights occurred regularly. A woman was raped. There was even a murder in the stands.

The number of policemen inside and outside the ballpark was increased. But fans became reluctant to park their cars and walk on the streets, as well as to sit in the stands. By 1969, the Phillies drew just 519,414, the team's lowest attendance since 1945.

As early as the 1950s, Bob Carpenter, who had lost more than $1 million in the sale of the stadium to Wolman, had wanted a new ballpark. Eventually, Veterans Stadium was completed at a cost of $52 million and scheduled to open in 1971.

Connie Mack Stadium had been in existence for 62 years and was the oldest major-league ballpark in the country. The final game was played there on October 1, 1970. Although just 1,186 fans had attended the previous day's game, 31,822 came to the finale.

Promoted as a "Farewell to Connie Mack Stadium," 5,000 slats used to repair seats were given out to fans. But from the fourth inning on, those slats, plus wrenches, hammers, and screwdrivers, were being used to rip away every possible piece of the park, including toilet seats.

The Phillies beat the Montreal Expos 2-1 in 10 innings, thereby finishing with a 1,205-1,340-13 record (.473) at the ballpark. After Tim McCarver singled home Oscar Gamble with the winning run, fans exploded onto the field, where they tore away anything they could.

Much of Connie Mack Stadium was destroyed by fire in 1971. In 1976, the city ordered the demolition of the remainder of the ballpark. With that came the end of the most storied stadium in Philadelphia sports history.

In its declining years, Connie Mack Stadium stood alone and lonely, with little left but the memories. Even the traffic along Lehigh Avenue was sparse.

In the late 1950s and early 1960s, as Phillies fortunes plummeted, crowds at Connie Mack Stadium were often miniscule. Sometimes, there would be no more than a few thousand in the stands. The 1961 team drew just 590,205 for the whole season.

THE END OF AN ICON

Unlike today, when starting pitchers warm up before the game in the team's bullpen, starters at Connie Mack Stadium warmed up alongside the dugout in front of the stands. Art Mahaffey is seen getting ready for a 1961 game that way before he went out and struck out 17 Chicago Cubs for a still-standing club record for most strikeouts in a nine-inning game. Later, he signed a ticket stub.

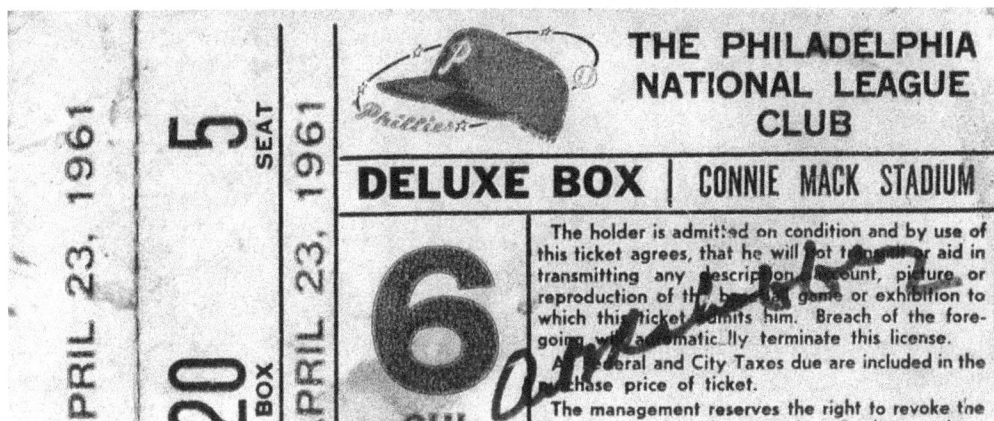

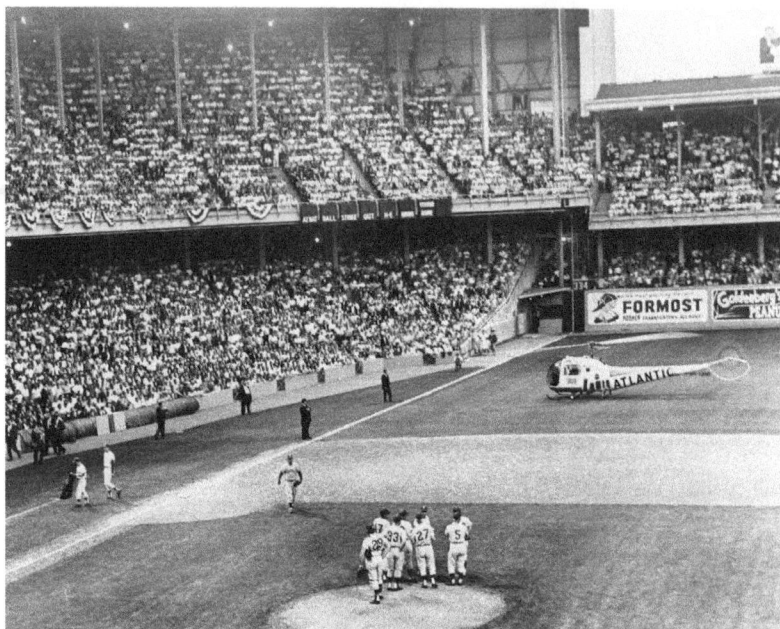

A big crowd did appear at Connie Mack Stadium in 1963, when a tribute was paid to the 1950 Whiz Kids. Reliever Jim Konstanty walked to the mound after being flown into the ballpark by helicopter.

Players used wire lockers and stools in the clubhouse. Phillies clubhouse manager Unk Russell (pictured here) kept the lockers supplied with clean uniforms. He, Ace Kessler, and Kenny Bush each served many years as clubhouse managers at Connie Mack Stadium.

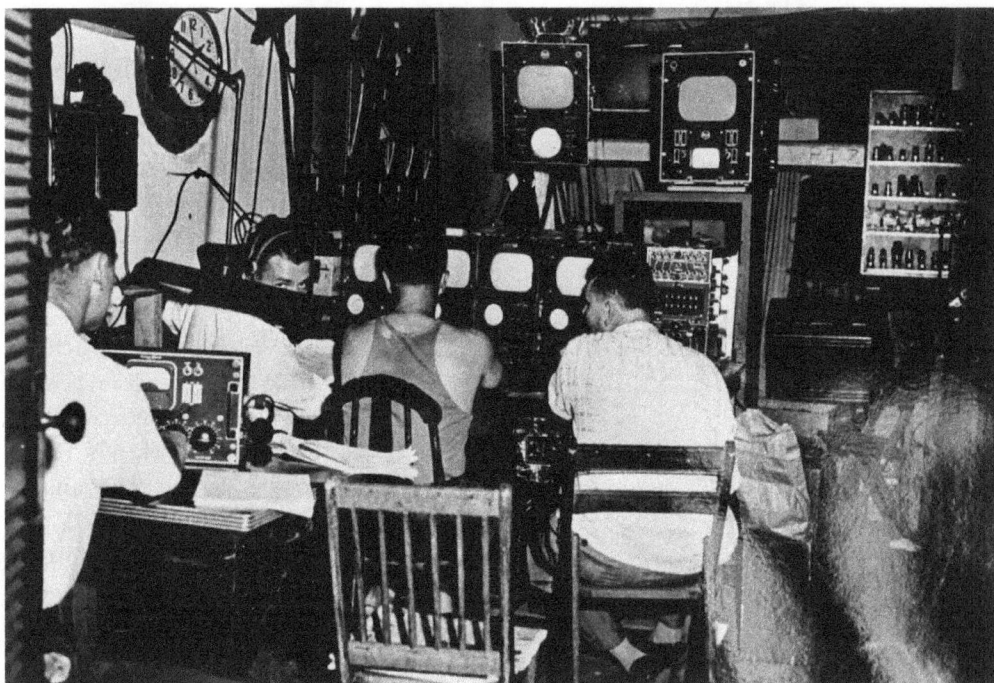

In the days before broadcasting a game became a highly technical science, the radio/television crew at Connie Mack Stadium worked in a small room to the side of the press box.

Except for the right-field wall, lower and upper decks surrounded the playing field at Connie Mack Stadium. In its final years, the ballpark seated 33,500. It was 331 feet down the line in right field, 340 to left, and 408 to dead center, beyond which the Phillies stored the batting cage used before games.

The mid-1960s saw a resurgence by the Phillies that was led by slugger Dick Allen, then known as Richie. Having come up through the Phils' farm system, Allen was named Rookie of the Year in 1964. Allen was sometimes involved in controversial issues, but his heavy hitting was unmatched during five stellar seasons with the Phillies that included the 1966 campaign when he hit .317 with 40 home runs and 112 RBI. Allen was noted for his mammoth clouts over the left-field roof. Once, one of them was measured as having traveled 529 feet.

Johnny Callison was another major player with the Phillies in the 1960s. Acquired in a trade, he was the only player to spend the entire decade with the team. A standout hitter and right fielder, Callison's most prominent moment occurred in the 1964 All-Star Game at Shea Stadium, when he hit a game-winning three-run homer in the bottom of the ninth inning off Dick Radatz.

THE END OF AN ICON

The top Phillies pitcher in the 1960s was Jim Bunning, who won 19 games in three straight seasons from 1964 to 1966 and 17 in 1967. Bunning became the first Phillies pitcher to hurl a perfect game, when he blanked the New York Mets in 1964 at Shea Stadium. Overall, he won 89 games during two stints with the Phillies. He was inducted into the Hall of Fame in 1996.

In 1964, the Los Angeles Dodgers' Sandy Koufax pitched the first no-hitter against the Phillies at Shibe Park/Connie Mack Stadium; it was one of four no-hitters registered by Koufax during his career. The Phillies were no-hit only two other times at Twenty-first Street and Lehigh Avenue (George Culver in 1968 and Bill Stoneman in 1969). No Phillies pitcher ever tossed a no-hitter at the ballpark.

Gene Mauch won the second-highest number of games and lost more games than any manager in Phillies history. Fans in front-row seats behind the home-team dugout on the third-base side could often hear the fiery skipper screaming at umpires.

When fans entered the ballpark through the main gate at Twenty-first Street and Lehigh Avenue, they walked into an open area where vendors sold scorecards and other items. Fans then traveled either upstairs or down one of two 14-foot-wide concourses to their seats. The concourses, on each side of the ballpark, passed the team clubhouses. (Temple University Urban Archives.)

THE END OF AN ICON

With a six-and-a-half game lead and just 12 games left to play, the 1964 Phillies appeared to be the forthcoming National League pennant-winner. World Series tickets were printed; a reserved seat in the upper deck would have cost $8. But a colossal collapse in which the Phils lost 10 straight games knocked them out of first place, rendering the tickets useless to a city of disbelieving fans.

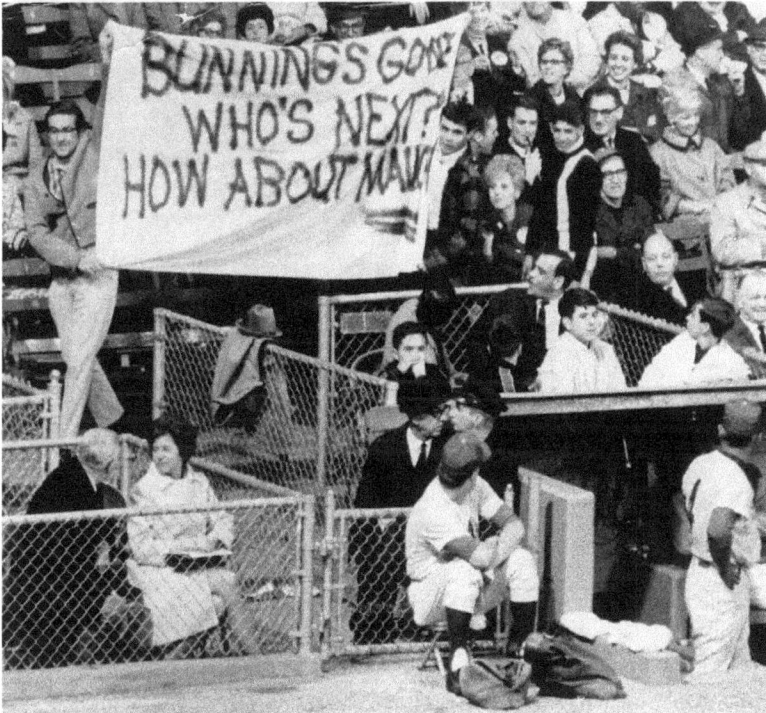

Phillies fans never hesitated to offer an opinion. They were known far and wide for their habit of booing things they did not like. Some even carried signs stating their views. It was often said that Shibe Park was noted for its "boo birds," its blocked views, its good beer and hot dogs, and its Sunday curfews.

Promotions and giveaways were frequent occurrences that attracted large numbers of fans. Bat days were especially popular; for 88¢, a fan could buy a ticket and get a free bat. Special days for school and scout groups also reeled in large numbers of fans.

A pre-game show brought laughing Phillies players out of the dugout. Those seen enjoying the festivities include Chris Short (back left) and Dallas Green (back right), Bobby Wine and Bill White (both in center), and coach George Myatt (right).

THE END OF AN ICON

Old-Timers' Games were a fixture at Connie Mack Stadium for many years. The last one took place in 1970, with the 1950 Phillies facing former members of the Philadelphia Athletics in a three-inning game. Before the game, Bob "Lefty" Grove (above right) waves to the crowd. To the left of him is Wally Moses. Others in the picture include Bob Johnson (far left) and Al Brancato (third from left). A scorecard (at right) marked the occasion.

OLD-TIMERS GAME
Phillies vs Athletics A's
CONNIE MACK STADIUM
July 25, 1970

The Phillies are honored to be able to bring back former members of their organization and representatives of Philadelphia's departed American League franchise the Athletics, for this Old-Timers Game.

For the record, the A's were in operation here from 1901 through 1954, when the franchise was sold to the late Arnold Johnson and transferred to Kansas City. It later moved to Oakland, current home of the Athletics.

The Philadelphia Athletics provided the city and the game with some of their finest baseball hours. Many of their great players, led by Hall of Fame pitcher Lefty Grove, are with us tonight. Jimmy Dykes, who is managing the Athletics' Old-Timers, was the man who succeeded the legendary Connie Mack as manager of the A's. Until then, 1951, Mr. Mack had been the only manager in the long history of the club.

Eddie Sawyer, who guided our "Whiz Kids" of 1950 to the National League pennant, most appropriately comes back as manager of the Phils' Old-Timers. The '50 champions form the nucleus of his squad, including the pitching meal-ticket, Robin Roberts. Roberts last year was voted, by fans, the "Greatest Ever" Phillies player. I have to agree.

We welcome you, Old-Timers. It is a thrill to have you back with us.

President

THE PHILADELPHIA PHILLIES

No.	No.
Harry Anderson	Robin Roberts
Richie Ashburn	Jack Sanford
Del Ennis	Eddie Sawyer
Solly Hemus	Andy Seminick
Ted Kazanski	Roy Sievers
Danny Litwhiler	Curt Simmons
Stan Lopata	Dick Sisler
Russ Meyer	Emil Verban
Bill Nicholson	Bucky Walters
Ken Raffensberger	

THE PHILADELPHIA ATHLETICS

No.		No.	
1	Jimmy Dykes	12	Spook Jacobs
2	Joe Astroth	14	Eddie Collins
3	Hal Wagner	15	Rube Walberg
4	Bob Johnson	18	Ferris Fain
5	Dick Siebert	19	Lou Brissie
6	Al Brancato	20	Joe Coleman
7	Roger Cramer	21	Chubby Dean
8	Wayne Ambler	34	Gus Zernial
9	Wally Moses	34	Bobby Shantz
10	Lefty Grove	35	Elmer Valo
11	George Earnshaw		

EDDIE SAWYER
ROBIN ROBERTS
CURT SIMMONS
RICHIE ASHBURN
BUCKY WALTERS
DEL ENNIS
ANDY SEMINICK

JIMMY DYKES
LEFTY GROVE
GEORGE EARNSHAW
RUBE WALBERG
ROGER CRAMER
BOB JOHNSON
FERRIS FAIN

In the ballpark's final years, advertising signs decorated the lower levels of the outfield walls. Small bullpens were located at the far ends of the foul lines. Gene Mauch moved the home team's bullpen from left to right field so he could keep an eye on his relievers as they warmed up. Ever the innovator, Mauch used a shift in which he placed four infielders on the right side of the diamond against certain left-handed pull hitters.

THE END OF AN ICON

1969
TAX EXEMPT
ENTER PRESS GATE

The *Phillies* Would be pleased to have

DELAWARE COUNTY DAILY TIMES✳✳✳✳✳

A FREQUENT VISITOR AT CONNIE MACK STADIUM
DURING THE NATIONAL LEAGUE SEASON

This pass is issued subject to the conditions set forth on the back hereof.

President.

434

Press passes in the 1960s were just cards carried in the wallets of the holders. The media entered the ballpark through a special gate before riding an elevator to the press level and crossing a ramp to the press box located between the lower and upper decks.

Fans attending the final game at Connie Mack Stadium on October 1, 1970, received a special certificate. As noted, more than 47 million fans saw major-league baseball games at the ballpark during its 62 years of existence.

1909 1970

October 1st, 1970

The Last Game at   Connie Mack Stadium

AFFIX SEAT COUPON HERE

PHILADELPHIA *phillies*   MONTREAL *expos*

This certifies that the last Major League baseball game played in Connie Mack Stadium was attended by: _____

Let it be known that in its sixty-two seasons, Connie Mack Stadium, formerly Shibe Park, played host to 47 million fans. The stadium, and its many great stars of the past and present, will be remembered by all who enjoy our national pastime.

R. R. M. CARPENTER, JR.
President, Philadelphia National League Club

The first game, April 12, 1909, Philadelphia A's vs. Boston. Philadelphia won, 8-1. Manager, Connie Mack. Attendance — 30,162.

Tri-State Printers, Inc., Phila., Pa.

Tim McCarver singled, stole second, and scored on a hit by Oscar Gamble in the 10th inning to give the Phillies a 2-1 win over the Montreal Expos in the final game at Connie Mack Stadium. Afterward, players raced to their clubhouses as fans stormed onto the field in search of souvenirs.

Much of the grandstand crowd dashed onto the field and grabbed anything they could as a memento of the old ballpark. Most of the field was torn up as fans pulled up pieces of grass and dirt.

THE END OF AN ICON

Whole rows of seats were carried away by fans, many of whom had brought hammers and wrenches to the game. By the end of the game, spectators had torn apart much of the interior of the stadium, even prying loose toilet-seat lids.

The day after the final game, there was not much left of the grandstands. Using tools as well as 5,000 wooden slats that the Phillies had given away as souvenirs, seats were ripped loose. Later, 1,500 usable seats were sent to the Phillies' farm team in Spartanburg, South Carolina, where they were used at the club's Duncan Park.

One thing fans were not able to dig up was home plate; groundskeeper John Godfrey got it the next day. Eventually, the plate was relocated to the new Veterans Stadium.

While the Phillies opened their 1971 season on the other side of the city at Veterans Stadium, youngsters from the surrounding neighborhood at Connie Mack Stadium appeared at the old ballpark to lament its closing. By then, workers had started to remove what was left of the playing field.

THE END OF AN ICON

Upon their departure from Connie Mack Stadium, the Phillies moved into a sparkling new $52-million ballpark in South Philadelphia named Veterans Stadium. Originally seating 56,371 for baseball, the multipurpose stadium had first been discussed in the mid-1950s. Also used by the Eagles and various other teams, the stadium served Philadelphia sports teams for 33 years.

A statue of Connie Mack that had originally stood at Reyburn Park, across the street from Connie Mack Stadium, was relocated to South Philadelphia, where it stood outside of Veterans Stadium. Since then, it has been relocated to a spot across from one of the entrances to Citizens Bank Park. (Chris Westcott.)

SHIBE PARK–CONNIE MACK STADIUM

Connie Mack Stadium was heavily damaged by a multi-alarm fire in August 1971. Virtually everything that could burn did. The fire took an especially heavy toll on the inside of the ballpark.

THE END OF AN ICON

Even the outside of Connie Mack Stadium had deteriorated badly by the mid-1970s, including the main entrance at Twenty-first Street and Lehigh Avenue.

Two years after the fire, Connie Mack Stadium still stood, an eerie reminder of its glorious history. Much of the parking lot was used by people at Dobbins Tech, which stood across Lehigh Avenue.

By order of the city government, the remains of Connie Mack Stadium were demolished in 1976. The ballpark was ripped apart by cranes slinging wrecking balls that knocked down everything that was left. The property was then sold to a developer.

THE END OF AN ICON

In the final stages of the demolition, all that remained was a small part of the area near the main entrance. Ultimately, the debris was cleared away, and the land where a ballpark once stood was reduced to a barren lot. A stoplight at the corner of Twenty-first Street and Lehigh Avenue was all that was left.

In the 1990s, there was still a bar on the spot where Quinn's Bar once attracted legions of fans at the corner of Twentieth Street and Lehigh Avenue. The row homes that notoriously sat behind the right-field wall were still there, too.

Over the years, a variety of plans were suggested for the use of the city block where Connie Mack Stadium stood. A hospital, a shopping center, and an industrial park were among the ideas. Finally, in 1990, Deliverance Evangelistic Church was built on the site. The church has a sanctuary that can seat 5,100, and its property covers the entire area where there once was a ballpark.

THE END OF AN ICON

ABOUT THE AUTHOR

Rich Westcott has served on the staffs of various newspapers and magazines in the Philadelphia area during more than 40 years as a writer and editor. He is the author of 22 previous books, the most recent being the *Philadelphia Phillies—Past and Present*.

Among his other books are *Back Again: The Story of the 2009 Phillies*; *The Mogul—Eddie Gottlieb, A Philadelphia Sports Legend and Pro Basketball Pioneer*; and *The Fightin' Phils—Oddities, Insights, and Untold Stories*. Other books include *The Phillies Encyclopedia* (with Frank Bilovsky), *Tales from the Phillies Dugout*; *Phillies Essential*; *Phillies '93—An Incredible Season*; *Philadelphia's Old Ballparks*; *A Century of Philadelphia Sports*; and *Veterans Stadium: Field of Memories*. Westcott also wrote *Mickey Vernon: The Gentleman First Baseman*, plus three books that are collections of interviews and profiles of some 120 former major-league baseball players. Other books include *Great Home Runs of the 20th Century*; *Winningest Pitchers—Baseball's 300-Game Winners*; and *No-Hitters—The 225 Games Between 1893 and 1999*.

Westcott was the founding owner and for 14 years the publisher and editor of *Phillies Report*, a newspaper covering the local major-league baseball team. He was also a member of a five-person committee and chief writer assigned to plan and produce the permanent interior historical exhibits displayed at the Phillies' Citizens Bank Park. Rich has also written for numerous national publications.

Considered the leading authority on Phillies history, Westcott has appeared in nine baseball documentaries, including four produced by Major League Baseball. He is president of the Philadelphia Sports Writers' Association, serves on the selection committee for the Phillies Hall of Fame, and is an advisor to the Philadelphia Sports Hall of Fame. He has also been a journalism instructor at La Salle and Temple Universities. Westcott has been inducted into three sports halls of fame.

Visit us at
arcadiapublishing.com